GW00891037

EDITOR: Maryanne Blacker

FOOD EDITOR: Pamela Clark

• • •

ART DIRECTOR: Robbylee Phelan

ARTISTS: Michael Howard, Kathleen Hunter

• • •

ASSISTANT FOOD EDITOR: Louise Patniotis

ASSOCIATE FOOD EDITOR: Enid Morrison

SENIOR HOME ECONOMISTS:
Kathy McGarry, Sophia Young

HOME ECONOMISTS: Angela Bresnahan, Annette Brien,
Janene Brooks, Karen Buckley, Caroline Jones, Justin Kerr,
Jodie Tilse, Lovoni Walker

EDITORIAL COORDINATOR: Elizabeth Hooper

KITCHEN ASSISTANT: Amy Wong

• • •

STYLISTS: Marie-Helene Clauzon, Carolyn Fienberg,
Jane Hann, Jacqui Hing, Cherise Koch

PHOTOGRAPHERS: Kevin Brown, Robert Clark,
Robert Taylor, Jon Waddy

• • •

HOME LIBRARY STAFF:

ASSISTANT EDITOR: Bridget van Tinteren

EDITORIAL COORDINATOR: Fiona Lambrou

• • •

ACP PUBLISHER: Richard Walsh

ACP DEPUTY PUBLISHER: Nick Chan

ACP CIRCULATION & MARKETING DIRECTOR:
Judy Kiernan

• • •

Produced by The Australian Women's Weekly Home Library.
Colour separations by Network Graphics Pty. Ltd. Sydney.
Cover separations by ACP Colour Graphics Pty Ltd, Sydney.
Printing by Hannanprint. Sydney. Published by ACP
Publishing Pty. Limited, 54 Park Street, Sydney.
◆ AUSTRALIA: Distributed by Network Distribution Company,
54 Park Street Sydney, (02) 282 8777.
◆ UNITED KINGDOM: Distributed in the U.K. by Australian
Consolidated Press (UK) Ltd, 20 Galowhill Rd, Brackmills,
Northampton NN4 7EE (01604) 760 456.
◆ CANADA: Distributed in Canada by Whitecap Books Ltd,
351 Lynn Ave, North Vancouver B.C. V7J 2C4 (604) 980 9852.
◆ NEW ZEALAND: Distributed in New Zealand by Netlink
Distribution Company, 17B Hargreaves St, Level 5,
College Hill, Auckland 1 (9) 302 7616.
◆ SOUTH AFRICA: Distributed in South Africa by Intermag,
PO Box 57394, Springfield 2137 (011) 493 3200.

• • •

Casseroles

Includes index.
ISBN 1 86396 043 0

1. Casserole Cookery. I. Title: Australian
Women's Weekly. (Series: Australian
Women's Weekly Home Library).

641.821

• • •

© A C P Publishing Pt. Limited 1995
ACN 053 273 546
This publication is copyright. No part of it may be
reproduced or transmitted in any form without the written
permission of the publishers.

• • •

COVER: Chicken with Mushrooms and Celeriac, page 17.
OPPOSITE: Pepper Casserole with Zucchini
and Beans, page 110.
BACK COVER: Braised Veal Rolls with Pasta
and Olives, page 79.

• • •

Casseroles

and other delicious one-pot wonders

Casseroles feature in every clever cook's repertoire; they are fuss-free, flavourful and always popular. Steaming one-pot wonders these days are brimming with many new flavour combinations, but traditional, hearty fare is just as tempting. Some of our recipes for chicken, seafood and vegetarian are really quick, taking under 30 minutes to cook. And to make this book even more helpful, there are ideas for cooking ahead and freezing, a bonus when you're too busy to cook during the week. Before you start, read our "Casserole Basics" on page 121 for handy hints and tips.

Pamela Clark
FOOD EDITOR

BRITISH & NORTH AMERICAN READERS: Please note that Australian cup and spoon measurements are metric. A quick conversion guide appears on page 127.
A glossary explaining unfamiliar terms and ingredients appears on page 122.

Chicken

In this super large chicken section you will find many fresh new styles for today with flavour combinations which will delight you. We have also included our best versions of some of the old favourites. Most of these recipes are deliciously quick, while some can be cooked in less than 30 minutes! Some full-flavoured dishes are also suitable for a slow cooker or pressure cooker, if you prefer.

HONEY AND ORANGE CHICKEN WITH CUMQUATS

1 cup (250ml) orange juice
2 tablespoons lemon juice
2 tablespoons honey
4 (1.4kg) chicken marylands
2 tablespoons vegetable oil
2 medium (300g) onions, sliced
2 cloves garlic, crushed
2 teaspoons sambal oelek
1 large (350g) red pepper, chopped
1½ teaspoons ground cumin
½ teaspoon ground turmeric
120g small cumquats
1 cup (250ml) chicken stock
2 teaspoons cornflour
1 tablespoon water
1 tablespoon chopped fresh mint

COUSCOUS
1½ cups (225g) couscous
1 tablespoon olive oil
1 cup (250ml) boiling water

Combine juices and honey in large bowl, add chicken; mix well. Cover, refrigerate several hours or overnight.

Drain chicken; reserve marinade. Pat chicken dry with absorbent paper. Heat oil in large shallow pan, add chicken, skin side down, cook until browned, then brown other side; remove from pan.

Remove all but 2 tablespoons of oil from pan. Add onions, garlic, sambal oelek, pepper, spices and cumquats, cook, stirring, until onions are soft. Add reserved marinade, stock and chicken to pan, simmer, covered, about 20 minutes or until chicken is tender. Turn chicken halfway through cooking. Remove chicken from pan, boil liquid until reduced by a third.

Just before serving, stir in blended cornflour and water, stir over heat until mixture boils and thickens slightly. Return chicken to pan, simmer until heated through; stir in mint. Serve with couscous.
Couscous: Combine couscous, oil and boiling water in heatproof bowl, cover, stand 5 minutes.
Serves 4.

■ Recipe can be made 3 hours ahead.
■ Storage: Covered, in refrigerator.
■ Freeze: Suitable.

♣ Microwave: Not suitable.
♣ Slow cooker: Not suitable.
♣ Pressure cooker: Not suitable.
♣ Conventional oven: Suitable.

RIGHT: Honey and Orange Chicken with Cumquats.

Fabric from Morris Home & Garden Wares.

CHICKEN SAUSAGES WITH BEANS

2 medium (400g) red peppers
1 tablespoon vegetable oil
800g chicken sausages
2 medium (300g) onions, sliced
3 cloves garlic, crushed
4 bacon rashers, chopped
440g can baked beans in tomato sauce
425g can tomatoes
1/4 cup (60ml) Worcestershire sauce
2 tablespoons chopped fresh parsley

Quarter peppers, remove seeds and membranes. Grill peppers, skin side up, until skin blisters and blackens. Peel away skin, chop peppers. Heat oil in large pan, add sausages, cook until browned. Remove from pan, cut sausages in half. Add onions to same pan with garlic and bacon, cook, stirring, until onions are soft and bacon lightly browned. Add beans, undrained crushed tomatoes, sauce, peppers and halved sausages, simmer, covered, 20 minutes. Serve sprinkled with parsley.
Serves 6.

■ Recipe can be made a day ahead.
■ Storage: Covered, in refrigerator.
■ Freeze: Suitable.

♣ Microwave: Not suitable.
♣ Slow cooker: Not suitable.
♣ Pressure cooker: Not suitable.
♣ Conventional oven: Suitable.

SEASONED CHICKEN WITH CREAMY SAGE SAUCE

8 (1.2kg) chicken thigh cutlets
1 tablespoon olive oil
1 medium (350g) leek, sliced
1 clove garlic, crushed
1/2 cup (125ml) dry white wine
1 cup (250ml) chicken stock
1/2 cup (125ml) cream
1 tablespoon chopped fresh sage
2 teaspoons seeded mustard
1 tablespoon cornflour
2 tablespoons water

SEASONING
2 teaspoons olive oil
1 small (80g) onion, sliced
1 clove garlic, crushed
200g minced pork and veal
1 cup (70g) stale breadcrumbs
1 tablespoon chopped fresh sage
1 egg yolk

Push seasoning under skin of cutlets, secure openings with toothpicks. Heat oil in large pan, add chicken in batches, cook until lightly browned; remove from pan. Drain excess oil from pan. Add leek and garlic to same pan, cook, stirring, until leek is soft. Return chicken to pan, add wine and stock, simmer, covered, about 30 minutes or until chicken is tender. Remove chicken from pan; discard toothpicks.

Add cream, sage, mustard and blended cornflour and water to pan, stir over heat until mixture boils and thickens slightly. Return chicken to pan, cook until heated through.

Seasoning: Heat oil in pan, add onion and garlic, cook, stirring, until onion is soft. Remove from heat, stir in remaining ingredients.
Serves 4.

■ Recipe can be made a day ahead.
■ Storage: Covered, in refrigerator.
■ Freeze: Suitable.

♣ Microwave: Seasoning suitable.
♣ Slow cooker: Not suitable.
♣ Pressure cooker: Not suitable.
♣ Conventional oven: Suitable.

LEFT: Chicken Sausages with Beans.
BELOW: Seasoned Chicken with Creamy Sage Sauce.

CHICKEN, DATE AND HONEY TAGINE

1 teaspoon salt
1 teaspoon cracked black pepper
½ teaspoon ground saffron
2 teaspoons ground cumin
8 (1.2kg) chicken thigh cutlets
30g butter
1 tablespoon olive oil
1 large (200g) onion, chopped
1 cinnamon stick
1½ cups (375ml) water
6 (150g) seedless fresh dates
2 teaspoons honey
¼ cup (40g) blanched almonds, toasted

SAFFRON COUSCOUS
2 cups (500ml) chicken stock
pinch ground saffron
2 cups (300g) couscous
40g butter

Rub combined salt, pepper, saffron and cumin onto chicken, cover, refrigerate 2 hours or overnight.

Heat butter and oil in large pan, add chicken, cook until browned; remove from pan. Drain all but 1 tablespoon of oil from pan, add onion and cinnamon to pan, cook, stirring, until onion is soft.

Return chicken to pan, add water, simmer, covered, about 30 minutes or until chicken is tender. Just before serving, add dates and honey, simmer, uncovered, 10 minutes or until slightly thickened. Serve tagine with saffron couscous, sprinkled with nuts.

Saffron Couscous: Boil stock in pan with saffron, remove from heat, stir in couscous, stand 5 minutes; fluff with a fork. Heat butter in pan, add couscous, cook, stirring, until combined.

Serves 4.

- Recipe can be made a day ahead.
- Storage: Covered, in refrigerator.
- Freeze: Tagine suitable. Couscous not suitable.

- Microwave: Not suitable.
- Slow cooker: Not suitable.
- Pressure cooker: Suitable.
- Conventional oven: Suitable.

LEFT: Chicken, Date and Honey Tagine.
RIGHT: African-Style Peanut, Okra and Tomato Gumbo.

Left: Food cover, cushion cover and servers from Morris Home & Garden Wares. Right: Setting from Morris Home & Garden Wares.

AFRICAN-STYLE PEANUT, OKRA AND TOMATO GUMBO

300g okra
2 tablespoons peanut oil
8 (800g) chicken thigh fillets, chopped
2 large (400g) onions, sliced
3 cloves garlic, crushed
1 teaspoon sambal oelek
5 medium (650g) tomatoes, peeled, seeded, chopped
¼ cup (60ml) tomato paste
⅓ cup (85g) crunchy peanut butter
1 large (300g) potato, chopped
2 cups (500ml) water

Trim stems from okra. Heat half the oil in large pan, add chicken in batches, cook, stirring, until browned; drain on absorbent paper. Heat remaining oil in same pan, add onions, garlic and sambal oelek, cook, stirring, until onions are soft. Return chicken to pan, add remaining ingredients, simmer, covered, about 30 minutes or until potato is tender.

Serves 4.

- Recipe best made close to serving.
- Freeze: Suitable.

- Microwave: Not suitable.
- Slow cooker: Suitable.
- Pressure cooker: Suitable.
- Conventional oven: Suitable.

MOROCCAN-STYLE CHICKEN WITH ALMONDS

1 cup (170g) raisins, chopped
3 green shallots, finely chopped
1 medium (150g) apple, peeled, cored, grated
1 teaspoon ground ginger
1/2 cup (35g) stale breadcrumbs
14 (1.5kg) chicken thigh fillets
1 tablespoon olive oil
1/3 cup (55g) blanched almonds, toasted
1/2 cup (125ml) orange juice
1/4 cup (60ml) plum jam
1/2 cup (125ml) dry white wine
1/2 teaspoon ground cinnamon
1 cup (250ml) chicken stock

Combine raisins, shallots, apple, ginger and breadcrumbs in bowl, spread level tablespoons of mixture onto each thigh fillet, roll up, secure with toothpicks. Heat oil in pan, add chicken in batches, cook until browned; remove from pan.

Combine remaining ingredients in same pan, bring to boil, return chicken to pan, simmer, uncovered, about 20 minutes or until chicken is tender. Remove toothpicks. Serve sprinkled with extra toasted almonds and shredded shallots, if desired.

Serves 6.

■ Recipe can be made a day ahead.
■ Storage: Covered, in refrigerator.
■ Freeze: Suitable.

♣ Microwave: Not suitable.
♣ Slow cooker: Not suitable.
♣ Pressure cooker: Not suitable.
♣ Conventional oven: Suitable.

ABOVE: Moroccan-Style Chicken with Almonds.
RIGHT: Herb-Seasoned Chicken with Beer.

Above: Dishes from Accoutrement.

HERB-SEASONED CHICKEN WITH BEER

8 (1.2kg) chicken drumsticks
plain flour
2 teaspoons vegetable oil
1 cup (250ml) beer
½ cup (125ml) chicken stock
1 tablespoon Worcestershire sauce
2 teaspoons cornflour
2 teaspoons water

HERB SEASONING
2 bacon rashers, chopped
¾ cup (45g) stale breadcrumbs
40g butter, melted
1 tablespoon chopped fresh oregano
1 tablespoon chopped fresh chives
2 teaspoons chopped fresh thyme
1 teaspoon seasoned pepper

Push herb seasoning under skin of drumsticks, toss in flour, shake away excess flour. Heat oil in pan, add chicken in batches, cook until browned. Return chicken to pan, add beer, stock and sauce, simmer, covered, about 20 minutes or until chicken is tender, stirring occasionally. Just before serving, add blended cornflour and water, cook, stirring, until sauce boils and thickens. Serve with pasta or rice, if desired.

Herb Seasoning: Heat pan, add bacon, cook, stirring, until browned; remove from heat, stir in remaining ingredients. Serves 4.

■ Seasoning can be made a day ahead. Casserole can be made 3 hours ahead.
■ Storage: Covered, in refrigerator.
■ Freeze: Suitable.

- Microwave: Bacon suitable.
- Slow cooker: Not suitable.
- Pressure cooker: Not suitable.
- Conventional oven: Suitable.

QUICK 'N' EASY CHICKEN WITH PISTACHIOS

1 tablespoon vegetable oil
18 (2kg) chicken thigh fillets
1 large (200g) onion, sliced
3 cloves garlic, crushed
1 teaspoon ground coriander
1 teaspoon ground turmeric
½ teaspoon ground cardamom
1 teaspoon ground cumin
2 teaspoons dried crushed chillies
2 teaspoons grated fresh ginger
1 tablespoon fish sauce
400ml can coconut milk
1 cup (250ml) chicken stock
⅓ cup (50g) shelled pistachios, toasted

Heat oil in large pan, add chicken in batches, cook until browned; remove from pan. Add onion, garlic, spices and ginger to same pan, cook, stirring, until onion is soft. Add sauce, coconut milk, stock and nuts, bring to boil, return chicken to pan, simmer, uncovered, about 30 minutes or until chicken is tender. Serves 8.

■ Recipe can be made a day ahead. Add nuts just before serving.
■ Storage: Covered, in refrigerator.
■ Freeze: Suitable.

🍄 Microwave: Not suitable.
🍄 Slow cooker: Not suitable.
🍄 Pressure cooker: Not suitable.
🍄 Conventional oven: Suitable.

SPICY CARIBBEAN-STYLE CHICKEN STEW

9 (1kg) chicken thigh fillets
2 teaspoons ground allspice
1 teaspoon ground cinnamon
pinch ground nutmeg
1 tablespoon chopped fresh thyme
¼ cup (60ml) olive oil
2 medium (300g) onions, sliced
2 cloves garlic, crushed
1 tablespoon grated fresh ginger
1 teaspoon sambal oelek
5 medium (650g) tomatoes, peeled, seeded, chopped
2 tablespoons brown sugar
2 teaspoons grated orange rind
2 tablespoons soy sauce
1 medium (400g) kumara, chopped
2 fresh corn cobs, sliced
⅔ cup (160ml) water
1½ tablespoons cornflour
1 bunch (500g) English spinach, shredded

Cut chicken into 2cm strips. Toss chicken in combined spices and thyme. Heat half the oil in pan, add chicken in batches, cook, stirring, until browned; drain on absorbent paper.

Heat remaining oil in same pan, add onions, garlic, ginger and sambal oelek, cook, stirring, until onions are soft. Add tomatoes, sugar, rind, sauce, kumara, corn, chicken and ½ cup (125ml) of the water, cook, covered, about 15 minutes or until chicken and vegetables are tender; remove cover, simmer 5 minutes.

Just before serving, stir in blended cornflour and remaining water, stir over heat until mixture boils and thickens slightly. Remove from heat, add spinach, stir until spinach is wilted. Serves 6.

■ Recipe can be made a day ahead.
■ Storage: Covered, in refrigerator.
■ Freeze: Suitable.

🍄 Microwave: Not suitable.
🍄 Slow cooker: Not suitable.
🍄 Pressure cooker: Not suitable.
🍄 Conventional oven: Suitable.

RIGHT: Spicy Caribbean-Style Chicken Stew.
BELOW: Quick 'n' Easy Chicken with Pistachios.

PROSCIUTTO-WRAPPED CHICKEN

8 (800g) chicken thigh fillets
¼ cup (20g) grated parmesan cheese
1 tablespoon chopped fresh oregano
4 small (200g) bocconcini cheese, halved
8 slices (120g) prosciutto
2 tablespoons olive oil
1 clove garlic, crushed
6 medium (780g) tomatoes, chopped
1 small (80g) onion, chopped
¼ cup (60ml) chicken stock
2 teaspoons balsamic vinegar
1 tablespoon chopped fresh parsley

Lightly pound fillets with a meat mallet. Sprinkle each fillet with some of the combined parmesan cheese and oregano, top with bocconcini cheese, roll up tightly; secure with toothpicks. Wrap prosciutto firmly around open ends of chicken to secure cheese.

Heat half the oil in pan, add chicken in batches, cook until browned all over; remove from pan. Heat remaining oil in same pan, add garlic, tomatoes and onion, cook, stirring, about 5 minutes or until tomatoes and onion are soft. Return chicken to pan, add stock and vinegar, simmer, covered, 10 minutes. Turn chicken, simmer, uncovered, about 10 minutes or until chicken is tender. Stir in parsley. Discard toothpicks. Serve with pasta, if desired.
Serves 4 to 6.

■ Recipe can be prepared a day ahead.
■ Storage: Covered, in refrigerator.
■ Freeze: Suitable.
♣ Microwave: Not suitable.
♣ Slow cooker: Not suitable.
♣ Pressure cooker: Not suitable.
♣ Conventional oven: Suitable.

ABOVE: Prosciutto-Wrapped Chicken.
ABOVE RIGHT: Green Chicken Curry with Vegetables.

GREEN CHICKEN CURRY WITH VEGETABLES

6 (1kg) single chicken breast fillets
2 tablespoons peanut oil
1 large (200g) onion, sliced
1 medium (200g) green pepper,
**   roughly chopped**
1 cup (250ml) chicken stock
280ml can coconut milk
1 dried lime leaf
1 bunch (360g) baby bok choy,
**   roughly chopped**
2 teaspoons cornflour
2 teaspoons water
¼ cup shredded fresh basil

CURRY PASTE
1 small fresh green chilli
2 tablespoons chopped fresh
**   lemon grass**
1 tablespoon grated fresh ginger
2 cloves garlic, crushed
1 tablespoon fish sauce
1 tablespoon palm sugar
1 teaspoon ground coriander
½ teaspoon ground cumin
½ teaspoon ground ginger

Cut each fillet into 3 pieces. Heat half the oil in pan, add chicken in batches, cook until browned; remove from pan. Heat remaining oil in same pan, add onion, pepper and curry paste, cook, stirring, until onion is soft. Return chicken to pan, add stock, coconut milk and lime leaf, simmer, uncovered, about 20 minutes or until chicken is tender, stirring occasionally. Just before serving, add bok choy and blended cornflour and water, cook, stirring, until mixture boils and thickens slightly. Stir in basil. Discard lime leaf before serving.

Curry Paste: Blend or process all ingredients until combined.

Serves 4.

■ Recipe best made close to serving.
■ Freeze: Not suitable.

♣ Microwave: Not suitable.
♣ Slow cooker: Not suitable.
♣ Pressure cooker: Not suitable.
♣ Conventional oven: Suitable.

CHICKEN CACCIATORE

4 (1.4kg) chicken marylands
plain flour
1 tablespoon olive oil
2 cloves garlic, crushed
4 slices (60g) pancetta, chopped
1 large (200g) onion, chopped
1 medium (200g) yellow pepper,
    chopped
3 medium (450g) tomatoes,
    peeled, chopped
½ cup (125ml) dry white wine
½ cup (125ml) tomato puree
2 teaspoons chopped fresh sage
1 teaspoon chopped fresh rosemary
1 bay leaf

Cut chicken through joint into 2 pieces. Toss chicken in flour; shake away excess flour. Heat oil in pan, add chicken in batches, cook until browned all over; drain on absorbent paper.

Drain all but 1 tablespoon of juices from pan, add garlic, pancetta, onion and pepper, cook, stirring, until onion is soft. Add tomatoes, wine and puree, simmer, uncovered, 2 minutes. Return chicken to pan, add herbs and bay leaf, simmer, covered, about 30 minutes or until chicken is tender. Discard bay leaf before serving.
Serves 4.

■ Recipe can be made a day ahead.
■ Storage: Covered, in refrigerator.
■ Freeze: Suitable.

● Microwave: Not suitable.
● Slow cooker: Not suitable.
● Pressure cooker: Not suitable.
● Conventional oven: Suitable.

CHICKEN CASSOULET

1 cup (200g) dried haricot beans
500g thick spicy Italian sausages
250g thick pork sausages
4 (900g) chicken thighs
4 (1kg) single chicken breasts on
    the bone
1 tablespoon vegetable oil
3 bacon rashers, sliced
2 cloves garlic, crushed
3 cloves
12 black peppercorns
1 stick celery, sliced
4 medium (480g) carrots, sliced
2 medium (300g) onions, sliced
½ cup (125ml) dry white wine
1.5 litres (6 cups) water
2 tablespoons tomato paste

Place beans in bowl, cover well with cold water, cover; stand overnight.

Drain beans. Add all the sausages to large pan of boiling water, boil, uncovered, 2 minutes; drain. Remove skin from all the chicken, cut breasts in half. Heat oil in flameproof casserole dish (5 litre/20 cup capacity), add chicken and sausages in batches, cook until browned; drain on absorbent paper, slice sausages. Add bacon to same dish, cook, stirring, until crisp; drain on absorbent paper.

Return chicken to dish with beans, garlic, cloves, peppercorns, celery, carrots, onions, wine, water and paste. Bake, covered, in moderate oven 1½ hours. Add sausages, cover, bake about 30 minutes or until sausages are cooked. Serve sprinkled with bacon.
Serves 6 to 8.

■ Recipe can be made a day ahead.
■ Storage: Covered, in refrigerator.
■ Freeze: Suitable.

● Microwave: Not suitable.
● Slow cooker: Suitable.
● Pressure cooker: Suitable.
● Cook-top: Suitable.

LEFT: Chicken Cacciatore.
BELOW: Chicken Cassoulet.

Left: China from Waterford Wedgwood.
Below: Serviettes and casserole dish from House.

INDIAN-STYLE CURRY WITH RICE DUMPLINGS

You will need to cook about ⅔ cup (130g) jasmine rice for this recipe.

1 tablespoon peanut oil
12 (1.3kg) chicken thigh fillets, quartered
2 large (400g) onions, sliced
2 cloves garlic, crushed
2 teaspoons grated fresh ginger
1 teaspoon cumin seeds
1 teaspoon caraway seeds
2 tablespoons mild curry powder
425g can tomatoes
½ cup (125ml) water
2 small chicken stock cubes
1 tablespoon chopped fresh coriander

RICE DUMPLINGS
2 cups cooked jasmine rice
1 egg yolk
1 tablespoon chopped fresh coriander
1 cup (70g) stale breadcrumbs

Heat oil in large pan, add chicken in batches, cook, stirring, until chicken is browned all over. Return chicken to pan, add onions, garlic, ginger, seeds and curry powder, cook, stirring, until fragrant. Add undrained crushed tomatoes, water and crumbled stock cubes, simmer, covered, 30 minutes. Gently stir in dumplings, cook, uncovered, without boiling, until dumplings are just heated through. Serve sprinkled with coriander.

Rice Dumplings: Process rice and egg yolk until rice is chopped and mixture combined. Transfer rice mixture to bowl, add remaining ingredients; mix well. Using damp hands, roll level tablespoons of mixture into balls.

Serves 6.

■ Curry and dumplings can be made a day ahead.
■ Storage: Covered, separately, in refrigerator.
■ Freeze: Suitable without dumplings.
♠ Microwave: Not suitable.
♠ Slow cooker: Not suitable.
♠ Pressure cooker: Not suitable.
♠ Conventional oven: Suitable.

BELOW: Indian-Style Curry with Rice Dumplings.
RIGHT: Chicken with Mushrooms and Celeriac.

Below: Copper tray, bowls and box from Pacific East India Company.

CHICKEN WITH MUSHROOMS AND CELERIAC

2 large (700g) red peppers
8 (1.2kg) chicken thigh cutlets
plain flour
1 tablespoon olive oil
1½ teaspoons caraway seeds
5 dried juniper berries
1 medium (630g) celeriac, chopped
250g button mushrooms, halved
1½ cups (375ml) chicken stock
1 tablespoon tomato paste
3 teaspoons cornflour
1 tablespoon water
1 tablespoon chopped fresh parsley

Quarter peppers, remove seeds and membranes. Grill peppers, skin side up, until skin blisters and blackens. Peel away skin, slice peppers into strips.

Toss chicken in flour; shake away excess flour. Heat oil in flameproof casserole dish (3 litre/12 cup capacity), add chicken in batches, cook until browned; drain on absorbent paper. Add seeds, berries, celeriac and mushrooms to dish, cook, stirring, until mushrooms are just soft. Return chicken to dish with peppers, stock and paste; mix well. Bake, covered, in moderate oven about 45 minutes or until chicken is tender.

Remove chicken from dish, stir in blended cornflour and water, stir over heat until mixture boils and thickens

slightly. Serve chicken with sauce, sprinkled with parsley.
Serves 4.

■ Recipe can be made a day ahead.
■ Storage: Covered, in refrigerator.
■ Freeze: Suitable.

♣ Microwave: Not suitable.
♣ Slow cooker: Suitable.
♣ Pressure cooker: Suitable.
♣ Cook-top: Suitable.

CHILLI TOMATO CHICKEN

12 (1.5kg) chicken "lovely legs"
plain flour
2 tablespoons olive oil
1 medium (150g) red Spanish
**   onion, sliced**
2 cloves garlic, crushed
2 tablespoons pine nuts
2 small fresh red chillies,
**   finely sliced**
3 bacon rashers, roughly chopped
3 medium (390g) tomatoes,
**   peeled, chopped**
1 cup (250ml) chicken stock
1/4 cup chopped fresh basil
1/4 cup (60ml) tomato paste
1/2 cup (125ml) dry red wine
1/2 cup (80g) seedless black olives

Toss chicken in flour, shake away excess flour. Heat oil in large pan, add chicken in batches, cook until browned; remove from pan. Add onion, garlic, nuts, chillies and bacon to same pan, cook, stirring, until onion is soft. Stir in tomatoes, stock, basil, paste, wine and olives. Add chicken, simmer, uncovered, about 45 minutes or until chicken is tender.
Serves 6.

■ Recipe can be made a day ahead.
■ Storage: Covered, in refrigerator.
■ Freeze: Suitable.

🌑 Microwave: Not suitable.
🌑 Slow cooker: Suitable.
🌑 Pressure cooker: Suitable.
🌑 Conventional oven: Suitable.

CHICKEN WITH RED BEANS

1 tablespoon vegetable oil
1 medium (150g) onion, chopped
2 medium (400g) red peppers,
**   chopped**
1 tablespoon sliced canned drained
**   jalapeno peppers**
2 cloves garlic, crushed
1/2 teaspoon chilli powder
1 teaspoon paprika
1 teaspoon ground coriander
1 teaspoon ground cumin
750g minced chicken
2 x 310g cans red kidney beans,
**   rinsed, drained**
425g can tomatoes
2 tablespoons tomato paste
1 tablespoon chopped fresh parsley

Heat oil in pan, add onion, red peppers, jalapenos and garlic, cook, stirring, until onion is soft. Stir in chilli powder, paprika, coriander and cumin, cook, stirring, until fragrant. Add chicken, cook, stirring, until browned. Add beans, undrained crushed tomatoes, paste and parsley, cook, covered, about 15 minutes or until slightly thickened.
Serves 6.

■ Recipe can be made a day ahead.
■ Storage: Covered, in refrigerator.
■ Freeze: Suitable.

🌑 Microwave: Not suitable.
🌑 Slow cooker: Not suitable.
🌑 Pressure cooker: Not suitable.
🌑 Conventional oven: Suitable.

LEFT: Chilli Tomato Chicken.
ABOVE: Chicken with Red Beans.

Left: China from Waterford Wedgwood.
Above: Rug and bowl from Morris Home
& Garden Wares.

MEDITERRANEAN-STYLE ROAST CHICKEN

Ask your poultry specialist shop to bone out the chicken for you, or follow the steps below.

1.6kg chicken
1 tablespoon olive oil
2 tablespoons plain flour
3 cups (750ml) chicken stock
12 baby (300g) onions
12 baby (450g) new potatoes
1 cup (160g) seedless black olives

SEASONING
1 large (350g) red pepper
2 teaspoons olive oil
4 slices (60g) prosciutto, chopped
4 green shallots, chopped
1 tablespoon chopped fresh parsley
2 teaspoons chopped fresh sage
300g minced chicken
1 cup (70g) stale breadcrumbs
½ cup (80g) pine nuts, toasted

Place chicken, breast side down, on board. Using poultry shears or a sharp knife, cut along each side of backbone; discard bone.

Scrape meat away from rib cage and breastbone; discard bones.

Spread chicken out flat. To remove thigh bone, cut along side of thigh bone to joint, hold end of bone and scrape away flesh. Cut bone away at joint; discard bone. Repeat with other thigh.

Top chicken with seasoning, fold sides and ends over seasoning, secure with toothpicks. Tie chicken securely with string at 3cm intervals, tie legs together.

Heat oil in baking dish, add chicken, cook until browned all over, remove from dish. Add flour to dish, stir over heat until bubbling, add stock gradually, stir until mixture boils and thickens. Return chicken to dish, add onions and potatoes, cover, bake in moderately hot oven 1 hour, remove cover, bake 20 minutes or until chicken is tender. Stir in olives. Stand chicken, covered, 10 minutes before carving.

Seasoning: Quarter pepper, remove seeds and membranes. Grill pepper, skin side up, until skin blisters and blackens. Peel away skin, chop pepper. Heat oil in pan, add prosciutto and shallots, cook until shallots are soft, stir in herbs. Combine minced chicken, breadcrumbs, pine nuts, shallot mixture and pepper in bowl; mix well.
Serves 4 to 6.

■ Chicken and seasoning can be prepared separately a day ahead.
■ Storage: Covered, in refrigerator.
■ Freeze: Not suitable.
♣ Microwave: Not suitable.
♣ Slow cooker: Not suitable.
♣ Pressure cooker: Not suitable.
♣ Cook-top: Not suitable.

LEFT: Mediterranean-Style Roast Chicken.

CREAMY CHICKEN WITH ASPARAGUS

6 (1kg) single chicken breast fillets, halved
plain flour
1½ tablespoons olive oil
2 sticks celery, chopped
10 (250g) spring onions, trimmed, halved
2 cloves garlic, crushed
45g packet cream of chicken soup mix
2½ cups (625ml) water
2 tablespoons drained green peppercorns
1 tablespoon French mustard
250g asparagus, chopped
¼ cup (60ml) cream
2 teaspoons chopped fresh thyme

Toss chicken in flour, shake away excess flour. Heat 1 tablespoon of the oil in pan, add chicken in batches, cook until browned; remove from pan. Heat remaining oil in same pan, add celery, onions and garlic, cook, stirring, until onions are soft.

Return chicken to pan, stir in soup mix, water, peppercorns and mustard, simmer, covered, about 20 minutes or until chicken is tender, stirring occasionally.

Add asparagus, cook, stirring, few minutes or until asparagus is tender. Stir in cream and thyme, simmer, uncovered, few minutes.
Serves 4.

■ Recipe can be made a day ahead.
■ Storage: Covered, in refrigerator.
■ Freeze: Suitable.
🖤 Microwave: Not suitable.
🖤 Slow cooker: Not suitable.
🖤 Pressure cooker: Not suitable.
🖤 Conventional oven: Suitable.

BELOW: Creamy Chicken with Asparagus.
RIGHT: Quick Thai-Style Chicken and Potatoes.

Right: Bowls and serviettes from Morris Home & Garden Wares; tiles from Country Floors.

QUICK THAI-STYLE CHICKEN AND POTATOES

1 tablespoon peanut oil
1 large (300g) red Spanish onion, sliced
1 tablespoon red curry paste
6 (600g) chicken thigh fillets
½ cup (125ml) chicken stock
18 baby (720g) new potatoes
1 cup (250ml) coconut milk
1 tablespoon lime juice
1 tablespoon fish sauce
1 tablespoon shredded fresh basil

Heat oil in pan, add onion and curry paste, cook, stirring, until onion is soft. Add chicken in batches, cook until browned. Return chicken to pan, add stock and potatoes, simmer, covered, about 20 minutes or until chicken and potatoes are tender. Stir in coconut milk, lime juice, sauce and basil, simmer, uncovered, 5 minutes.
Serves 4.

■ Recipe best made just before serving.
■ Freeze: Not suitable.
🖤 Microwave: Not suitable.
🖤 Slow cooker: Not suitable.
🖤 Pressure cooker: Not suitable.
🖤 Conventional oven: Not suitable.

CHICKEN, PEPPER AND CAPER STEW

8 (1.2kg) chicken drumsticks
1/4 cup (35g) plain flour
1 teaspoon paprika
2 tablespoons olive oil
1 medium (200g) red pepper, roughly chopped
1 medium (200g) yellow pepper, roughly chopped
1 medium (150g) onion, roughly chopped
100g button mushrooms, halved
2 cloves garlic, crushed
1 3/4 cups (430ml) chicken stock
1/4 cup (60ml) dry white wine
2 bay leaves
2 tablespoons drained tiny capers

Remove skin from chicken. Toss chicken in combined flour and paprika, shake away excess flour mixture.

Heat half the oil in pan, add chicken in batches, cook until browned all over; remove from pan. Heat remaining oil in same pan, add peppers, onion, mushrooms and garlic, cook, stirring, until onion is soft. Return chicken to pan, add stock, wine, bay leaves and capers, simmer, covered, 20 minutes, stirring occasionally. Remove cover, simmer 10 minutes or until chicken is tender. Discard bay leaves before serving.
Serves 4.

■ Recipe can be made a day ahead.
■ Storage: Covered, in refrigerator.
■ Freeze: Suitable.

♣ Microwave: Not suitable.
♣ Slow cooker: Suitable.
♣ Pressure cooker: Suitable.
♣ Conventional oven: Suitable.

CURRIED LEMON CHICKEN

12 (2kg) chicken thigh cutlets
plain flour
2 tablespoons vegetable oil
1 medium (350g) leek, chopped
2 sticks celery, sliced
2 cloves garlic, crushed
2 teaspoons mild curry powder
1 tablespoon lemon juice
1 large (350g) green pepper, chopped
250g button mushrooms
3 cups (750ml) chicken stock

Remove skin from chicken. Toss chicken in flour; shake away excess flour. Heat oil in flameproof casserole dish (3 litre/12 cup capacity), add chicken in batches, cook until browned; drain on absorbent paper. Add leek, celery, garlic and curry powder to same dish, cook, stirring, until leek is soft. Add juice, pepper and mushrooms, cook, stirring, 2 minutes or until liquid has evaporated. Add chicken and stock, mix gently. Bake, covered, in moderate oven about 1 hour or until chicken is tender.
Serves 4 to 6.

■ Recipe can be made a day ahead.
■ Storage: Covered, in refrigerator.
■ Freeze: Suitable.

♣ Microwave: Not suitable.
♣ Slow cooker: Suitable.
♣ Pressure cooker: Suitable.
♣ Cook-top: Suitable.

LEFT: Chicken, Pepper and Caper Stew.
RIGHT: Curried Lemon Chicken.

Left: Plates from House.

CHICKEN THYME STEW WITH POLENTA DUMPLINGS

12 (2kg) chicken thigh cutlets
1/4 cup (60ml) olive oil
2 medium (600g) eggplants, chopped
6 small (480g) onions
4 medium (520g) tomatoes, chopped
1/2 cup (125ml) chicken stock
1 tablespoon red wine vinegar
1/4 cup (40g) seedless black olives
2 teaspoons chopped fresh thyme
70g feta cheese, crumbled

POLENTA DUMPLINGS
3 1/2 cups (875ml) chicken stock
1 cup (170g) polenta
40g butter
1/2 cup (40g) grated parmesan cheese
1 egg, lightly beaten
1/4 cup chopped fresh parsley

Remove skin from chicken. Heat 1 tablespoon of the oil in flameproof casserole dish (3 litre/12 cup capacity), add chicken in batches, cook until browned; remove from dish. Heat remaining oil in same dish, add eggplants and onions, then tomatoes, cook, stirring, 5 minutes. Return chicken to dish with stock, vinegar, olives and thyme. Bring to boil, then bake, uncovered, in moderate oven 1 hour. Top with rounded tablespoons of dumpling mixture, sprinkle with cheese, bake,
uncovered, in moderate oven about 20 minutes or until dumplings are cooked.
Polenta Dumplings: Bring stock to boil in pan, gradually whisk in polenta, simmer, stirring, about 15 minutes or until very thick. Remove from heat, stir in butter, cheese, egg and parsley.
Serves 6.

■ Stew can be made a day ahead; dumplings best made just before serving.
■ Storage: Covered, in refrigerator.
■ Freeze: Stew suitable.
🥄 Microwave: Not suitable.
🥄 Slow cooker: Not suitable.
🥄 Pressure cooker: Not suitable.
🥄 Cook-top: Chicken mixture suitable.

ABOVE: Chicken Thyme Stew with Polenta Dumplings.
RIGHT: Braised Chicken with Lentils and Sage.

Right: Setting from Barbara's Storehouse.

BRAISED CHICKEN WITH LENTILS AND SAGE

8 (1.2kg) chicken drumsticks
plain flour
2 tablespoons olive oil
2 large (360g) carrots, roughly chopped
1 medium (200g) onion, roughly chopped
1 1/2 cups (375ml) chicken stock
1/2 cup (125ml) tomato puree
4 medium (480g) zucchini, sliced
1/2 cup (100g) red lentils
1 tablespoon chopped fresh sage

Remove skin from chicken. Toss chicken in flour, shake away excess flour. Heat half the oil in pan, add chicken in batches, cook until browned; remove from pan. Heat remaining oil in same pan, add carrots and onion, cook, stirring, until onion is soft. Return chicken to pan, add stock and puree, simmer, covered, 15 minutes. Stir in zucchini, lentils and sage, simmer, covered, 15 minutes or until lentils are tender, stirring occasionally.

Serves 4.
■ Recipe can be made 3 hours ahead.
■ Storage: Covered, in refrigerator.
■ Freeze: Suitable.
🥄 Microwave: Not suitable.
🥄 Slow cooker: Suitable.
🥄 Pressure cooker: Suitable.
🥄 Conventional oven: Suitable.

COQ AU VIN

1.5kg chicken pieces
plain flour
40g butter
2 cloves garlic, crushed
3 bacon rashers, chopped
10 (250g) spring onions, trimmed
200g Swiss brown mushrooms,
**   halved**
2 tablespoons brandy
1 cup (250ml) dry red wine
1 cup (250ml) chicken stock
1 sprig fresh parsley
2 teaspoons chopped fresh thyme
1 bay leaf
2 tablespoons tomato paste

Toss chicken in flour; shake away excess flour. Heat butter in large pan, add chicken, cook until browned all over; drain on absorbent paper. Drain all but 1 tablespoon of juices from pan, add garlic, bacon, onions and mushrooms, cook, stirring, until onions are lightly browned. Return chicken to pan, add brandy, wine, stock, herbs, bay leaf and paste, simmer, covered, 30 minutes or until chicken is tender. Remove chicken from pan, simmer sauce until slightly thickened. Discard bay leaf before serving. Serve chicken with sauce. Serves 4.

- ■ Recipe can be made a day ahead.
- ■ Storage: Covered, in refrigerator.
- ■ Freeze: Not suitable.

- ♣ Microwave: Not suitable.
- ♣ Slow cooker: Not suitable.
- ♣ Pressure cooker: Not suitable.
- ♣ Conventional oven: Suitable.

CHICKEN GUMBO

400g okra
12 (2kg) chicken thigh cutlets
2 tablespoons olive oil
2 medium (300g) onions, chopped
3 cloves garlic, crushed
1 medium (200g) green pepper,
**   chopped**
1 medium (200g) red pepper,
**   chopped**
1½ teaspoons Cajun seasoning
½ teaspoon ground cumin
¼ teaspoon cayenne pepper
2 bay leaves
2 cups (500ml) chicken stock
2 x 425g cans tomatoes
2 teaspoons Worcestershire sauce

Trim stems from okra. Remove skin from chicken. Heat oil in pan, add chicken in batches, cook until browned all over; drain on absorbent paper. Add onions, garlic and okra to same pan, cook, stirring, until onions are soft. Return chicken to pan, add peppers, spices and bay leaves, cook, stirring, until fragrant. Add stock, undrained crushed tomatoes and sauce; simmer, covered, 1 hour. Simmer, uncovered, 10 minutes or until thickened slightly. Discard bay leaves before serving. Serves 6.

- ■ Recipe can be made a day ahead.
- ■ Storage: Covered, in refrigerator.
- ■ Freeze: Suitable.

- ♣ Microwave: Not suitable.
- ♣ Slow cooker: Suitable.
- ♣ Pressure cooker: Suitable.
- ♣ Conventional oven: Suitable.

CHICKEN WITH LEMON AND ROSEMARY

1 tablespoon olive oil
18 (2kg) chicken thigh fillets
3 cloves garlic, crushed
1 cup (250ml) chicken stock
½ cup (125ml) dry white wine
1 teaspoon grated lemon rind
2 tablespoons lemon juice
1 tablespoon chopped fresh rosemary
2 teaspoons cornflour
1 tablespoon water
¼ cup (60ml) cream

Heat oil in pan, add chicken in batches, cook until browned; remove from pan. Add garlic, stock, wine, rind, juice and rosemary to same pan, bring to boil. Return chicken to pan, simmer, uncovered, about 20 minutes or until chicken is tender, remove chicken from pan. Add blended cornflour and water to pan, stir over heat until sauce boils and thickens. Reduce heat, add cream and chicken, stir until hot.
Serves 6 to 8.

■ Recipe best made just before serving.
■ Freeze: Suitable.
♣ Microwave: Not suitable.
♣ Slow cooker: Not suitable.
♣ Pressure cooker: Not suitable.
♣ Conventional oven: Suitable.

LEFT: Chicken Gumbo.
ABOVE LEFT: Coq au Vin.
ABOVE: Chicken with Lemon and Rosemary.

Above left: China from Waterford Wedgwood; black wooden bowl and tray from Morris Home & Garden Wares. Above: Plate from Country Floors.

HOT AND SPICY CHICKEN AND KUMARA

12 (2kg) chicken thigh cutlets
1/4 cup (35g) plain flour
2 teaspoons ground cumin
2 teaspoons paprika
2 teaspoons ground turmeric
2 tablespoons vegetable oil
1 medium (150g) onion, quartered
1 medium (120g) carrot, sliced
2 cloves garlic, crushed
1 teaspoon sambal oelek
1 1/2 cups (375ml) chicken stock
1/4 cup chopped fresh coriander
1 medium (400g) kumara, chopped
1/4 cup (60ml) sour cream

Remove skin from chicken, toss chicken in combined flour and spices, reserve remaining flour mixture. Heat oil in pan, add chicken in batches, cook until browned; remove from pan. Add onion, carrot, garlic and sambal oelek to same pan, cook, stirring, until onion is soft. Add reserved flour mixture to pan, stir until mixture is dry and grainy. Remove from heat, gradually stir in stock, stir over heat until mixture boils and thickens slightly.

Return chicken to pan, simmer, uncovered, 20 minutes. Add coriander and kumara, simmer, uncovered, 15 minutes or until kumara is just tender. Stir in cream.

Serves 6.
- ■ Recipe can be made a day ahead; add sour cream after reheating.
- ■ Storage: Covered, in refrigerator.
- ■ Freeze: Suitable.

- ♣ Microwave: Not suitable.
- ♣ Slow cooker: Not suitable.
- ♣ Pressure cooker: Not suitable.
- ♣ Conventional oven: Suitable.

CHICKEN MARENGO

6 (1kg) chicken thigh cutlets
6 (900g) chicken drumsticks
2 tablespoons olive oil
250g button mushrooms
250g flat mushrooms, sliced
2 medium (300g) onions, sliced
2 cloves garlic, crushed
2 tablespoons plain flour
1/2 cup (125ml) chicken stock
1/2 cup (125ml) dry white wine
1 tablespoon tomato paste
425g can tomatoes
1 tablespoon chopped fresh parsley

Remove skin from chicken. Heat oil in flameproof casserole dish (3.5 litre/14 cup capacity), add chicken in batches, cook until browned; drain on absorbent paper. Drain all but 1 tablespoon of the oil from dish, add all mushrooms, onions and garlic to dish, cook, stirring, until onions are soft. Add blended flour and stock, then wine, paste and undrained crushed tomatoes, stir over heat until mixture boils and thickens; return chicken to dish. Bake, covered, in moderate oven about 1 hour or until chicken is tender. Serve sprinkled with parsley.

Serves 6.
- ■ Recipe can be made a day ahead.
- ■ Storage: Covered, in refrigerator.
- ■ Freeze: Not suitable.

- ♣ Microwave: Not suitable.
- ♣ Slow cooker: Suitable.
- ♣ Pressure cooker: Suitable.
- ♣ Cook-top: Suitable.

LEFT: Hot and Spicy Chicken and Kumara.
ABOVE: Chicken Marengo.

Left: Copper and box from Pacific East India Company. Above: Casserole dish and serviettes from The Bay Tree Kitchen Shop.

Beef

Fragrant with herbs, spices and seasonings, our beef recipes make fabulous eating in casseroles, pot roasts, saucy stews — even pies! Most beef recipes are suitable for a slow cooker or pressure cooker, and the soft, leafy vegetables, such as spinach, are added just before serving. Any thickening with flour is done after the meat is cooked.

BEEF DIANE

1kg beef chuck steak
1 tablespoon olive oil
4 cloves garlic, crushed
1 medium (150g) onion, chopped
425g can tomatoes
½ cup (125ml) water
2 small beef stock cubes
2 tablespoons Worcestershire sauce
½ cup (125ml) cream
**2 tablespoons chopped
    fresh parsley**
1 tablespoon brandy

Cut beef into 3cm pieces. Heat oil in large pan, add beef in batches, cook, stirring, until browned. Return beef and any juices to pan, add garlic and onion, cook, stirring, until onion is soft.

Add undrained crushed tomatoes, water, crumbled stock cubes and sauce, simmer, covered, about 1½ hours or until beef is tender. Add remaining ingredients, simmer, uncovered, about 5 minutes or until thickened slightly. Serve with pasta and sprinkled with extra chopped parsley, if desired. Serves 4 to 6.

■ Recipe can be made a day ahead.
■ Storage: Covered, in refrigerator.
■ Freeze: Suitable; stir in cream, parsley and brandy just before serving.
♣ Microwave: Not suitable.
♣ Slow cooker: Suitable.
♣ Pressure cooker: Suitable.
♣ Conventional oven: Suitable.

RIGHT: Beef Diane.

Plates from Art House.

PEPPERCORN GARLIC BEEF WITH BABY VEGETABLES

1 tablespoon olive oil
**900g piece fresh eye of
    beef silverside**
½ cup (125ml) dry red wine
½ cup (125ml) water
2 small beef stock cubes
2 sprigs fresh thyme
2 cloves garlic, sliced
1 teaspoon black peppercorns
20 baby (500g) onions
1 bunch (400g) baby carrots
12 baby (480g) new potatoes, halved

Heat oil in large pan, add beef, cook until browned all over. Add wine, water, crumbled stock cubes, thyme, garlic, peppercorns and onions, simmer, covered, 30 minutes. Add carrots and potatoes, simmer, covered, about 30 minutes or until vegetables and beef are tender. Remove beef and vegetables from pan; keep warm.

Simmer pan juices until reduced to about ½ cup (125ml) liquid; strain. Serve sliced beef and vegetables with pan juices.
Serves 6.

- Recipe best made just before serving.
- Freeze: Not suitable.
- Microwave: Not suitable.
- Slow cooker: Suitable.
- Pressure cooker: Suitable.
- Conventional oven: Suitable.

BOEUF BOURGUIGNONNE

1kg beef chuck steak
2 tablespoons vegetable oil
60g butter
10 baby (250g) onions
400g button mushrooms
3 bacon rashers, chopped
1 clove garlic, crushed
¼ cup (35g) plain flour
1 cup (250ml) beef stock
1 cup (250ml) dry red wine
2 bay leaves
1 tablespoon brown sugar
3 teaspoons chopped fresh oregano

Cut beef into 3cm pieces. Heat half the oil in pan, add beef in batches, cook until browned; remove from pan. Heat remaining oil and butter in same pan, add onions, mushrooms, bacon and garlic, cook, stirring, until onions are lightly browned. Stir in flour, stir over heat until mixture is browned.

Remove from heat, gradually stir in stock and wine; stir over heat until sauce boils and thickens. Return beef and any juices to pan, add bay leaves, sugar and oregano. Simmer, covered, about 2 hours or until beef is tender, stirring occasionally. Discard bay leaves.
Serves 4 to 6.

- Recipe can be made a day ahead.
- Storage: Covered, in refrigerator.
- Freeze: Suitable.
- Microwave: Not suitable.
- Slow cooker: Suitable.
- Pressure cooker: Suitable.
- Conventional oven: Suitable.

LEFT: Peppercorn Garlic Beef with Baby Vegetables.
BELOW: Boeuf Bourguignonne.

Left: Tiles from Country Floors.

BEEF IN RED WINE SAUCE WITH ROASTED TOMATOES

8 medium (600g) egg tomatoes, halved
1/4 cup (60ml) olive oil
2 cloves garlic, crushed
1 teaspoon sugar
4 bacon rashers, sliced
1 medium (120g) carrot, sliced
1 medium (150g) onion, chopped
12 baby (300g) onions
250g button mushrooms
1.5kg beef chuck steak, chopped
2 tablespoons plain flour
3 cups (750ml) dry red wine
1 bay leaf
2 tablespoons cornflour
1 cup (250ml) water
2 tablespoons chopped fresh parsley

Place tomatoes, cut side up, on oven tray. Combine 1 tablespoon of the oil with garlic, brush tomatoes with oil mixture, sprinkle with sugar. Bake, uncovered, in moderate oven about 30 minutes or until tomatoes are tender.

Heat 1 tablespoon of the remaining oil in flameproof casserole dish (3 litre/12 cup capacity), add bacon, cook, stirring, until lightly browned; drain on absorbent paper. Add carrot and chopped onion to same dish, cook, stirring, until lightly browned; remove from dish. Add baby onions and mushrooms to same dish, cook, stirring, until onions are lightly browned; remove from dish.

Heat remaining oil in same dish, add beef in batches, cook, stirring, until browned. Return beef to dish, add flour, cook, stirring, 2 minutes. Add wine, bacon, chopped onion mixture and bay leaf to dish, bake, covered, in moderate oven about 1 hour. Stir in mushrooms and baby onions, then blended cornflour and water. Bake, covered, about 45 minutes or until beef is tender. Discard bay leaf; gently stir in tomatoes and parsley.

Serves 8.

■ Recipe can be made a day ahead.
■ Storage: Covered, in refrigerator.
■ Freeze: Suitable; stir in tomatoes and parsley after reheating.
♣ Microwave: Not suitable.
♣ Slow cooker: Suitable.
♣ Pressure cooker: Suitable.
♣ Cook-top: Suitable.

RIGHT: Steak and Kidney Pie.
BELOW: Beef in Red Wine Sauce with Roasted Tomatoes.

Right: Setting from Accoutrement.
Below: Dish from House.

STEAK AND KIDNEY PIE

300g beef ox kidneys
1.5kg beef chuck steak, chopped
2 medium (300g) onions, sliced
1 cup (250ml) beef stock
1 tablespoon soy sauce
¼ cup (35g) plain flour
½ cup (125ml) water
2 sheets ready-rolled puff pastry
1 egg, lightly beaten

Remove fat from kidneys, chop kidneys finely. Combine kidneys, beef, onions, stock and sauce in pan, simmer, covered, about 1 hour or until beef is tender.

Stir blended flour and water into beef mixture, stir until mixture boils and thickens, transfer to ovenproof dish (1.5 litre/ 6 cup capacity). Cut pastry into 6cm rounds, overlap rounds on beef mixture, brush with egg. Bake in moderate oven about 15 minutes or until browned.

Serves 6.

◼ Recipe can be prepared a day ahead.
◼ Storage: Covered, in refrigerator.
◼ Freeze: Beef suitable.

🍶 Microwave: Not suitable.
🍶 Slow cooker: Beef suitable.
🍶 Pressure cooker: Beef suitable.
🍶 Conventional oven: Beef suitable.

BEEF AND THREE POTATO HOT POT

2kg beef chuck steak, chopped
plain flour
¼ cup (60ml) vegetable oil
2 large (400g) onions, chopped
4 bacon rashers, chopped
2 teaspoons beef stock powder
1 litre (4 cups) water
1 small (250g) kumara, chopped
4 baby (160g) new potatoes
200g white sweet potato, chopped
2 tablespoons chopped fresh thyme
1 tablespoon tomato paste

Toss beef in flour; shake away excess flour. Heat half the oil in flameproof dish (2.5 litre/10 cup capacity), add onions and bacon, cook, stirring, until onions are soft; remove from dish. Heat remaining oil in same dish, add beef in batches, cook until browned. Return onion mixture and beef to dish, stir in stock powder and water, bake, covered, in moderate oven 1 hour. Add kumara, all the potatoes and thyme, cover, bake 1 hour or until beef is tender. Stir in paste, serve sprinkled with parsley, if desired.

Serves 8.

- ■ Recipe can be made a day ahead.
- ■ Storage: Covered, in refrigerator.
- ■ Freeze: Suitable.
- ♣ Microwave: Not suitable.
- ♣ Slow cooker: Suitable.
- ♣ Pressure cooker: Suitable.
- ♣ Cook-top: Suitable.

OXTAIL STEW

2kg chopped oxtail
plain flour
60g ghee
2 large (400g) onions, sliced
2 cloves garlic, crushed
2 teaspoons chopped
**   fresh rosemary**
¼ cup (60ml) dry red wine
2 large (360g) parsnips, sliced
2 medium (240g) carrots, sliced
3 cups (750ml) beef stock
1 teaspoon freshly ground
**   black pepper**
2 medium (240g) zucchini, sliced
1 cup (250ml) tomato puree
1 tablespoon chopped fresh parsley

Toss oxtail in flour, shake away excess flour. Heat ghee in large pan, add oxtail in batches, cook, stirring, until well browned all over; drain on absorbent paper. Add onions, garlic and rosemary to same pan, cook, stirring, until onions are soft.

Add wine, cook, stirring, until liquid is reduced by half. Return oxtail to pan, add parsnips, carrots, stock and pepper, cook, covered, 1¼ hours. Add zucchini, puree and parsley, cook, uncovered, 20 minutes or until oxtail is tender.
Serves 6.

- ■ Recipe best made a day ahead.
- ■ Storage: Covered, in refrigerator.
- ■ Freeze: Suitable.
- ♣ Microwave: Not suitable.
- ♣ Slow cooker: Suitable.
- ♣ Pressure cooker: Suitable.
- ♣ Conventional oven: Suitable.

ABOVE: Beef and Three Potato Hot Pot.
RIGHT: Oxtail Stew.

Above: Bowl from Accoutrement; tiles from Country Floors. Right: Setting from Accoutrement.

CHILLI BEEF AND BEANS

1.5kg beef chuck steak
1 tablespoon vegetable oil
1 large (200g) onion, chopped
3 cloves garlic, crushed
1 teaspoon ground cumin
1 teaspoon chilli powder
**1 medium (200g) green pepper,
    chopped**
**2 x 310g cans red kidney beans,
    rinsed, drained**
425g can tomato puree
425g can tomatoes
1 teaspoon dried oregano leaves
1/4 cup (60ml) corn relish
1 beef stock cube
1 teaspoon sugar

Cut beef into 3cm pieces. Heat oil in flameproof casserole dish (2.5 litre/ 10 cup capacity), add beef in batches, cook, stirring, until browned; remove from dish. Add onion, garlic and spices to same dish, cook, stirring, until onion is soft. Return beef to dish, add pepper, beans, puree, undrained crushed tomatoes, oregano, relish, crumbled stock cube and sugar. Bring to boil, then bake, covered, in moderately slow oven about 2 hours or until beef is tender. Serves 6.

■ Recipe can be made a day ahead.
■ Storage: Covered, in refrigerator.
■ Freeze: Suitable.

● Microwave: Not suitable.
● Slow cooker: Suitable.
● Pressure cooker: Suitable.
● Cook-top: Suitable.

FAMILY BEEF CASSEROLE

2 tablespoons vegetable oil
2kg beef chuck steak, chopped
2 medium (300g) onions, sliced
2 medium (240g) carrots, sliced
3 cloves garlic, crushed
1/4 cup chopped fresh parsley
1/4 cup (60ml) tomato paste
2 teaspoons French mustard
1 cup (250ml) dry red wine
1 cup (250ml) beef stock
1 egg, lightly beaten

SCONE TOPPING
2 cups (300g) self-raising flour
30g butter, chopped
1/4 cup chopped fresh parsley
3/4 cup (180ml) milk, approximately

Heat oil in flameproof casserole dish (2.5 litre/10 cup capacity), add beef in batches, cook until browned; remove from dish. Add onions, carrots and garlic to same dish, cook, stirring, until onions are soft. Return beef to dish, stir in parsley, paste, mustard, wine and stock, bake, covered, in slow oven about 1 3/4 hours or until beef is tender.

Place scone topping on hot beef mixture, brush with egg, bake, uncovered, in moderately hot oven about 15 min-

utes or until scones are browned and cooked through. Serve sprinkled with extra chopped parsley, if desired.
Scone Topping: Sift flour into bowl, rub in butter, stir in parsley and enough milk to mix to a soft dough. Turn dough onto lightly floured surface, knead lightly until smooth. Press dough out to 2cm thickness, cut into 5cm rounds.
Serves 6 to 8.

■ Beef can be prepared a day ahead. Scone topping best made just before serving.
■ Storage: Covered, in refrigerator.
■ Freeze: Beef suitable.

● Microwave: Not suitable.
● Slow cooker: Beef suitable.
● Pressure cooker: Beef suitable.
● Cook-top: Beef suitable.

LEFT: Chilli Beef and Beans.
ABOVE: Family Beef Casserole.

Left: Setting from Morris Home & Garden Wares.
Above: Dish from Accoutrement.

BEEF AND VEGETABLES WITH BEER

1½ tablespoons vegetable oil
1.5kg rolled roast of beef brisket
2 large (360g) carrots, chopped
2 large (360g) parsnips, chopped
6 baby (150g) onions
6 baby (240g) new potatoes
2 x 375ml cans beer

Heat oil in baking dish, add beef, cook until lightly browned all over; remove from dish. Add vegetables to dish, cook, stirring, until browned all over. Return beef to dish, add beer, bake, covered, in moderately hot oven 45 minutes. Remove vegetables to flat oven tray, cover loosely with foil, return to oven.

Turn beef, bake, uncovered, about 30 minutes or until beef is cooked through. Remove beef from dish, wrap in foil. Place baking dish over heat, simmer, uncovered, until liquid is reduced to about 1 cup (250ml). Serve sliced beef with vegetables and sauce.
Serves 6.

■ Recipe best made just before serving.
■ Freeze: Not suitable.
🌑 Microwave: Not suitable.
🌑 Slow cooker: Not suitable.
🌑 Pressure cooker: Not suitable.
🌑 Cook-top: Not suitable.

LEFT: Beef and Vegetables with Beer.

Servers from Orson & Blake; tiles from Country Floors.

BEEF WITH SALAMI, RED PEPPER AND OLIVES

2 tablespoons olive oil
1.5kg beef blade steak, chopped
1 medium (150g) onion, chopped
2 cloves garlic, crushed
3 teaspoons chopped fresh thyme
1 medium (200g) red pepper,
    chopped
60g sliced salami, sliced
425g can tomato puree
½ cup (125ml) water
2 sticks (200g) pepperoni, sliced
⅓ cup (50g) seedless black olives

CRISPY CHEESE TOAST
½ French-style bread stick
½ cup (60g) grated tasty
    cheddar cheese

Heat oil in large pan, add beef in batches, cook, stirring, until browned; remove from pan. Add onion, garlic, thyme, pepper and salami to same pan, cook, stirring, until onion is soft. Return beef to pan, add puree and water, simmer, covered, about 1 hour or until beef is tender. Stir in pepperoni and olives, cook, stirring, until heated through and thickened slightly. Serve topped with crispy cheese toast.

Crispy Cheese Toast: Cut bread diagonally into 1cm slices, grill on 1 side. Turn bread, sprinkle with cheese, grill until cheese is melted.
Serves 6.

■ Beef can be made a day ahead. Toast best made just before serving.
■ Storage: Covered, in refrigerator.
■ Freeze: Beef suitable.
● Microwave: Not suitable.
● Slow cooker: Beef suitable.
● Pressure cooker: Beef suitable.
● Conventional oven: Beef suitable.

RIGHT: Beef Patty Casserole with Potato Topping.
BELOW: Beef with Salami, Red Pepper and Olives.

Below: Tiles from Country Floors.

BEEF PATTY CASSEROLE WITH POTATO TOPPING

2 tablespoons olive oil
1 tablespoon cumin seeds
2 large (400g) onions, finely chopped
2 cloves garlic, crushed
800g minced beef
¼ cup (25g) packaged breadcrumbs
1 egg, lightly beaten
2 x 425g cans tomatoes
½ cup (125ml) tomato paste
1 tablespoon sugar

POTATO TOPPING
5 large (1.5kg) potatoes, chopped
3 cloves garlic, crushed
60g butter, chopped
1 cup (80g) grated parmesan cheese
¼ cup (60ml) cream

Heat half the oil in large pan, add seeds, cook, stirring, until fragrant. Add onions and garlic, cook, stirring, until onions are soft; remove from pan. Combine beef, half the onion mixture, breadcrumbs and egg in bowl; mix well. Shape ¼ cups of mixture into patties. Heat remaining oil in same pan, add patties in batches, cook until browned on both sides; drain on absorbent paper.

Combine remaining onion mixture, undrained crushed tomatoes, paste and sugar in bowl; mix well. Place patties in single layer in ovenproof dish (3 litre/ 12 cup capacity), add tomato mixture, spread with potato topping. Bake, uncovered, in moderately hot oven about 1 hour or until top is browned.

Potato Topping: Boil, steam or micro-wave potatoes and garlic until tender; drain. Mash potatoes with butter, cheese and cream.
Serves 6 to 8.

- Beef and tomato mixture can be made a day ahead.
- Storage: Covered, in refrigerator.
- Freeze: Suitable.
- Microwave: Potatoes suitable.
- Slow cooker: Not suitable.
- Pressure cooker: Not suitable.
- Cook-top: Not suitable.

CHILLI CON CARNE WITH CORNMEAL SAGE SCONES

1kg beef chuck steak
2 tablespoons olive oil
2 medium (300g) onions,
**   finely chopped**
3 cloves garlic, crushed
3 teaspoons ground cumin
1 teaspoon ground coriander
1 teaspoon chilli powder
1 tablespoon chopped fresh oregano
2 x 425g cans tomatoes
1 tablespoon beef stock powder
2 teaspoons sugar
1 cup (250ml) water
310g can red kidney beans,
**   rinsed, drained**

CORNMEAL SAGE SCONES
1 cup (150g) self-raising flour
½ cup (85g) cornmeal
½ cup (40g) grated parmesan
**   cheese**
1½ tablespoons chopped fresh sage
¼ cup (60ml) olive oil
½ cup (125ml) water

Cut beef into 2cm pieces. Heat half the oil in flameproof casserole dish (3 litre/ 12 cup capacity), add beef in batches, cook until browned; drain on absorbent paper. Heat remaining oil in same dish, add onions, garlic, spices and oregano, cook, stirring, until onions are soft. Add undrained crushed tomatoes, stock powder, sugar, beef and water, simmer, covered, about 1 hour or until beef is tender.

Stir beans into beef mixture, top with scones. Bake, uncovered, in moderately hot oven about 30 minutes or until scones are cooked through.

Cornmeal Sage Scones: Combine sifted flour, cornmeal, cheese and sage in bowl, add oil and water; mix to a soft dough. Knead dough on floured surface until smooth. Roll dough to 1cm thickness, cut into 4cm rounds.

Serves 6 to 8.

- Beef can be made a day ahead.
- Storage: Covered, in refrigerator.
- Freeze: Beef suitable.
- Microwave: Not suitable.
- Slow cooker: Beef suitable.
- Pressure cooker: Beef suitable.
- Conventional oven: Beef suitable.

LEFT: Chilli con Carne with Cornmeal Sage Scones.
BELOW: Meatballs and Risoni in Tomato Sauce.

Left: Moroccan plate and bowl from The Bay Tree Kitchen Shop. Below: Plate from The Bay Tree Kitchen Shop.

MEATBALLS AND RISONI IN TOMATO SAUCE

750g minced beef
1 clove garlic, crushed
⅓ cup chopped fresh parsley
2 green shallots, chopped
1 cup (70g) stale breadcrumbs
1 egg, lightly beaten
vegetable oil for shallow-frying
425g can tomatoes
300g can Tomato Supreme
1½ cups (375ml) beef stock
½ cup (110g) risoni pasta

Combine beef, garlic, parsley, shallots, breadcrumbs and egg in bowl; mix well. Shape ¼ cups of mixture into balls, shallow-fry in hot oil until browned; drain on absorbent paper. Combine meatballs, undrained crushed tomatoes, Tomato Supreme and stock in ovenproof dish (3 litre/12 cup capacity), bake, covered, in moderate oven 45 minutes. Stir in risoni, bake, covered, 20 minutes or until risoni is tender.

Serves 4 to 6.

- Recipe can be made a day ahead.
- Storage: Covered, in refrigerator.
- Freeze: Suitable.
- Microwave: Not suitable.
- Slow cooker: Suitable.
- Pressure cooker: Suitable.
- Cook-top: Suitable.

COUNTRY-STYLE BEEF AND MUSHROOMS

2 large (700g) red peppers
2 tablespoons olive oil
1.5kg beef blade steak, chopped
20g butter
2 cloves garlic, crushed
1 medium (620g) fennel bulb, sliced
200g button mushrooms, quartered
200g Swiss brown mushrooms, halved
200g shitake mushrooms, sliced
3¼ cups (810ml) beef stock
½ cup (100g) barley
1 bunch (500g) English spinach, shredded

Quarter peppers, remove seeds and membranes. Grill peppers, skin side up, until skin blisters and blackens. Peel away skin, cut peppers into thin strips.

Heat half the oil in large pan, add beef in batches, cook, stirring, until browned; remove from pan.

Heat remaining oil and butter in same pan, add garlic, fennel and mushrooms, cook, stirring, until fennel is tender. Return beef to pan, add peppers, stock and barley, simmer, covered, about 1 hour or until beef is tender. Add spinach, stir until just wilted.

Serves 6 to 8.

■ Recipe can be made a day ahead; add spinach just before serving.
■ Storage: Covered, in refrigerator.
■ Freeze: Beef mixture suitable; add spinach just before serving.
🍖 Microwave: Not suitable.
🍖 Slow cooker: Suitable.
🍖 Pressure cooker: Suitable.
🍖 Conventional oven: Suitable.

PROSCIUTTO AND BEEF ROLL

1.7kg piece of beef chuck steak
4 slices (60g) prosciutto
2 tablespoons olive oil
10 baby (250g) onions
12 baby (480g) new potatoes
1 cup (250ml) dry red wine
½ cup (125ml) beef stock
425g can tomatoes, drained, chopped
1 sprig fresh thyme
1 sprig fresh parsley
1 sprig fresh rosemary
2 fresh sage leaves
1 tablespoon cornflour
1 tablespoon water

Place beef, cut side up, on board, top with prosciutto, roll up firmly. Secure with string at 2cm intervals. Heat oil in baking dish, add beef, cook until browned all over; remove from dish. Add onions and potatoes to dish, cook, stirring, until lightly browned. Return beef to dish, add wine, stock and tomatoes.

Place herbs in a piece of muslin, tie securely with string. Add herbs to dish. Bake, covered, in slow oven about 3 hours or until beef is tender. Baste several times during cooking.

Remove beef and vegetables from dish, add blended cornflour and water to pan juices, stir over heat until mixture boils and thickens. Discard herbs. Serve sliced beef with vegetables and sauce.
Serves 6 to 8.

■ Recipe can be prepared a day ahead.
■ Storage: Covered, in refrigerator.
■ Freeze: Suitable; thicken with cornflour just before serving.
🍖 Microwave: Not suitable.
🍖 Slow cooker: Suitable.
🍖 Pressure cooker: Suitable.
🍖 Cook-top: Suitable.

ABOVE: Country-Style Beef and Mushrooms.
RIGHT: Prosciutto and Beef Roll.

CHILLI MARINATED BEEF IN COCONUT CURRY SAUCE

1.5kg beef chuck steak, chopped
40g ghee
2 medium (400g) red peppers, chopped
2 medium (300g) onions, chopped
½ cup (125ml) beef stock
½ cup (125ml) coconut milk
1 cinnamon stick
5 dried curry leaves
1 tablespoon chopped fresh coriander

MARINADE
⅓ cup (80ml) white vinegar
2 small fresh red chillies, sliced
2 tablespoons tomato paste
1 tablespoon chopped fresh coriander
2 cloves garlic, crushed
3 cardamom pods, crushed
2 teaspoons cumin seeds
1 teaspoon ground turmeric

Combine beef and marinade in bowl; mix well. Cover, refrigerate several hours or overnight.

Heat half the ghee in pan, add beef in batches, cook, stirring, until browned; remove from pan. Heat remaining ghee in same pan, add peppers and onions, cook, stirring, until onions are soft. Return beef to pan, add stock, coconut milk, cinnamon and curry leaves, simmer, covered, 1 hour, stirring occasionally.

Remove cover, simmer about 30 minutes or until beef is tender. Discard cinnamon stick and curry leaves; stir in coriander. Serve with steamed or boiled rice, if desired.
Marinade: Combine all ingredients in bowl; mix well.
Serves 6 to 8.

- ■ Recipe can be made a day ahead.
- ■ Storage: Covered, in refrigerator.
- ■ Freeze: Suitable.

- ♣ Microwave: Not suitable.
- ♣ Slow cooker: Suitable.
- ♣ Pressure cooker: Suitable.
- ♣ Conventional oven: Suitable.

FRUITY BEEF AND EGGPLANT TAGINE

1 medium (300g) eggplant
coarse cooking salt
1 tablespoon olive oil
½ teaspoon ground cinnamon
¼ teaspoon ground turmeric
½ teaspoon ground ginger
¼ teaspoon ground cumin
¼ teaspoon ground coriander
1kg beef chuck steak, chopped
1 medium (150g) onion, grated
2 cloves garlic, crushed
425g can tomatoes, drained
3 cups (750ml) beef stock
2 strips lemon rind
1 cinnamon stick
1 cup (170g) seedless prunes
2 tablespoons chopped fresh coriander
1 tablespoon sesame seeds, toasted

Cut eggplant into 1cm slices, place slices in colander, sprinkle with salt; stand 30 minutes. Rinse slices under cold water; drain on absorbent paper. Cut eggplant slices into quarters.

Heat oil in pan, add ground spices and beef, cook, stirring, until browned. Add onion and garlic, cook, stirring, 5 minutes. Stir in crushed tomatoes, stock, rind and cinnamon, simmer, covered, about 1 hour or until beef is tender. Add eggplant and prunes, simmer, uncovered, 30 minutes. Discard rind and cinnamon stick, stir in half the fresh coriander. Serve sprinkled with remaining fresh coriander and sesame seeds. Serve with couscous or rice, if desired.
Serves 4 to 6.

- ■ Recipe can be made a day ahead.
- ■ Storage: Covered, in refrigerator.
- ■ Freeze: Suitable.

- ♣ Microwave: Not suitable.
- ♣ Slow cooker: Suitable.
- ♣ Pressure cooker: Suitable.
- ♣ Conventional oven: Suitable.

LEFT: Fruity Beef and Eggplant Tagine.
BELOW: Chilli Marinated Beef in Coconut Curry Sauce.

Left: Plates from Morris Home & Garden Wares.
Below: Bowl and tiles from Country Floors; basket from Pacific East India Company.

EGGPLANT, BEEF AND BROAD BEAN PIE

1 large (500g) eggplant
coarse cooking salt
1kg beef chuck steak
1 tablespoon olive oil
2 large (400g) onions, sliced
2 cloves garlic, crushed
2 medium (260g) tomatoes, chopped
1/4 cup (60ml) dry red wine
250g frozen broad beans,
    thawed, peeled
2 tablespoons chopped fresh basil
1 small beef stock cube
1/2 cup (80g) seedless black olives
1 sheet ready-rolled puff pastry
1 egg yolk
1 tablespoon milk

Cut eggplant into 3cm pieces, place in colander, sprinkle with salt, stand 30 minutes. Rinse eggplant under cold water; drain on absorbent paper. Cut beef into 3cm pieces.

Heat oil in large pan, add beef in batches, cook until browned. Return beef and any juices to pan, add onions and garlic, cook, stirring, until onions are soft. Add tomatoes, wine and eggplant, simmer, covered, about 1 1/2 hours or until beef is tender. Stir in beans, basil, crumbled stock cube and olives; cool.

Spoon beef mixture into deep oven-proof dish (2.5 litre/10 cup capacity). Cover dish with pastry, trim edges, decorate with pastry scraps, if desired. Brush pastry with combined egg yolk and milk. Bake in moderately hot oven about 30 minutes or until browned.

Serves 4 to 6.

- Recipe can be made a day ahead.
- Storage: Covered, in refrigerator.
- Freeze: Beef suitable.
- Microwave: Not suitable.
- Slow cooker: Beef suitable.
- Pressure cooker: Beef suitable.
- Conventional oven: Suitable.

RIGHT: Spare Ribs in Oregano Mushroom Sauce.
BELOW: Eggplant, Beef and Broad Bean Pie.

SPARE RIBS IN OREGANO MUSHROOM SAUCE

1.5kg beef spare ribs
plain flour
¼ cup (60ml) olive oil
1 clove garlic, crushed
1 tablespoon chopped fresh oregano
2 large (400g) onions, sliced
3 medium (600g) potatoes, chopped
250g button mushrooms
3 cups (750ml) beef stock
1 bunch (20) baby carrots
2 tablespoons tomato paste

Toss ribs in flour; shake away excess flour. Heat 2 tablespoons of the oil in large pan, add ribs in batches, cook until browned all over; drain on absorbent paper. Heat remaining oil in same pan, add garlic, oregano and onions, cook, stirring, until onions are soft. Add potatoes, mushrooms and stock. Return ribs to pan, cook, covered, 1¼ hours. Add carrots and paste, cook, uncovered, about 10 minutes or until carrots are tender.
Serves 6.

■ Recipe can be made a day ahead.
■ Storage: Covered, in refrigerator.
■ Freeze: Suitable.

● Microwave: Not suitable.
● Slow cooker: Suitable.
● Pressure cooker: Suitable.
● Conventional oven: Suitable.

Lamb

Casserole cooking is ideal for lamb,
giving extra time to bring out the distinctive,
delicate taste that always makes lamb so special.
Most of the recipes in this section are suitable
for a slow cooker or pressure cooker.
And most are suitable to cook and freeze ahead;
any thickening with flour is done just
before serving. Some recipes use
lamb stock, but if this is not available,
chicken or beef stock can be substituted.

LAMB WITH ROSEMARY AND VEGETABLES

4 (1kg) lamb leg chops
2 cloves garlic, crushed
1 tablespoon vegetable oil
1 medium (350g) leek, chopped
4 baby (100g) onions, halved
2 medium (250g) parsnips, chopped
1 medium (400g) kumara, chopped
1/2 cup (125ml) dry red wine
1/2 cup (125ml) beef stock
2 tablespoons tomato paste
2 medium (240g) zucchini, chopped
2 teaspoons chopped fresh
    rosemary

Trim fat from chops. Rub garlic over chops. Heat oil in pan, add chops, cook until well browned. Add leek, onions, parsnips, kumara, wine, stock and paste, simmer, covered, 1 hour, stirring occasionally. Stir in zucchini and rosemary, simmer, covered, 30 minutes or until chops are tender.
Serves 4.

■ Recipe can be made a day ahead.
■ Storage: Covered, in refrigerator.
■ Freeze: Suitable.

♣ Microwave: Not suitable.
♣ Slow cooker: Suitable.
♣ Pressure cooker: Suitable.
♣ Conventional oven: Suitable.

RIGHT: Lamb with Rosemary and Vegetables.

Tiles from Country Floors.

LAMB AND ARTICHOKE STEW

3 medium (800g) globe artichokes
1/4 cup (60ml) lemon juice
1/4 cup (60ml) olive oil
1 large (200g) onion, sliced
1.5kg diced lamb
plain flour
2 1/2 cups (625ml) chicken stock
1 teaspoon grated lemon rind
2 medium (240g) carrots, sliced
1 cup (150g) frozen broad beans,
    thawed, peeled
1 tablespoon tomato paste
1 tablespoon chopped fresh dill
3/4 cup (125g) seedless black olives

Remove tough outer leaves from artichokes; trim tips of remaining leaves with scissors. Cut artichokes in half. Place artichokes and juice in pan of boiling water, simmer, uncovered, about 25 minutes or until tender; drain.

Heat 1 tablespoon of the oil in pan, add onion, cook, stirring, until soft; remove from pan. Toss lamb in flour, shake away excess flour. Heat remaining oil in same pan, add lamb in batches, cook until browned. Return lamb to pan with onion, stock and rind, simmer, uncovered, 45 minutes, stirring occasionally. Add carrots, simmer, uncovered, 10 minutes. Add beans and artichokes, simmer, uncovered, 15 minutes or until lamb and vegetables are tender. Stir in paste, dill and olives.

Serves 6.

- Recipe can be made a day ahead.
- Storage: Covered, in refrigerator.
- Freeze: Suitable.
- Microwave: Not suitable.
- Slow cooker: Suitable.
- Pressure cooker: Suitable.
- Conventional oven: Suitable.

RIGHT: Lamb Shanks with Madeira and Olive Sauce.
BELOW: Lamb and Artichoke Stew.

Below: Le Creuset casserole dish from The Bay Tree Kitchen Shop.

LAMB SHANKS WITH MADEIRA AND OLIVE SAUCE

1 teaspoon vegetable oil
250g pepperoni, sliced
8 (2kg) lamb shanks
4 medium (600g) onions, chopped
8 cloves garlic, peeled
¼ cup seedless black olives, finely chopped
2 tablespoons tomato paste
6 medium (450g) egg tomatoes, halved
2 cups (500ml) beef stock
½ cup (125ml) Madeira
2 teaspoons dried rosemary leaves
1 tablespoon cornflour
2 tablespoons water

Heat oil in flameproof casserole dish (3 litre/12 cup capacity), add pepperoni, cook, stirring, until browned; drain on absorbent paper. Add lamb in batches, cook until browned; remove from dish. Drain all but 1 tablespoon of oil from dish, add onions and garlic, cook, stirring, until onions are soft.

Return pepperoni and lamb to dish, add olives, paste, tomatoes, stock, Madeira and rosemary, bake, uncovered, in moderate oven 1¼ hours or until lamb is tender. Stir in blended cornflour and water, cook, stirring, until mixture boils and thickens.
Serves 6 to 8.

■ Recipe can be made a day ahead.
■ Storage: Covered, in refrigerator.
■ Freeze: Suitable; thicken with cornflour just before serving.
🍴 Microwave: Not suitable.
🍴 Slow cooker: Suitable.
🍴 Pressure cooker: Suitable.
🍴 Cook-top: Suitable.

GARLIC AND ROSEMARY LAMB POT ROAST

2 x 900g boned rolled lamb shoulders
4 cloves garlic, halved
4 small sprigs fresh rosemary
2 tablespoons olive oil
10 baby (250g) onions
12 baby (480g) new potatoes
½ bunch (10) baby carrots
½ cup (125ml) chicken stock
1 cup (250ml) dry white wine
3 (180g) finger eggplants, thickly sliced
425g can tomatoes
2 tablespoons sour cream

Using the point of a knife, cut small slits in lamb and insert garlic pieces and tiny sprigs of rosemary. Heat oil in flame-proof casserole dish (4 litre/16 cup capacity), add lamb, cook until browned all over. Add onions, potatoes, carrots, stock and wine, bake, covered, in moderately slow oven 2 hours. Add eggplants and undrained pureed tomatoes, bake, uncovered, about 30 minutes or until lamb is tender.

Remove lamb and vegetables from dish; keep warm. Bring pan juices to the boil, simmer, uncovered, until reduced to about 1½ cups (375ml). Stir in sour cream. Serve sliced lamb with vegetables and sauce.

Serves 8.

- ■ Recipe best made close to serving.
- ■ Freeze: Suitable.
- ♣ Microwave: Not suitable.
- ♣ Slow cooker: Suitable.
- ♣ Pressure cooker: Suitable.
- ♣ Cook-top: Suitable.

ABOVE: Garlic and Rosemary Lamb Pot Roast.
RIGHT: Spicy Coconut Lamb.

Right: Hand-painted tin from Morris Home & Garden Wares.

SPICY COCONUT LAMB

40g butter
4 dried curry leaves
2 medium (300g) onions, sliced
½ teaspoon chilli powder
1 teaspoon ground turmeric
1 teaspoon ground cumin
2 teaspoons ground coriander
5 cloves garlic, crushed
3 teaspoons grated fresh ginger
1kg diced lamb
2 tablespoons brown vinegar
425g can tomatoes
2½ cups (625ml) water
4 cardamom pods, bruised
1 cinnamon stick
2 strips lemon rind
4 small (480g) potatoes, chopped
4 (240g) finger eggplants, chopped
¼ cup (30g) packaged
   ground almonds
¾ cup (180ml) coconut milk

Heat butter in pan, add curry leaves, stir 2 minutes. Add onions, chilli powder, ground spices, garlic and ginger, cook, stirring, until fragrant. Add lamb, stir until lightly browned. Add vinegar, undrained crushed tomatoes, water, cardamom, cinnamon and rind; simmer, covered, 30 minutes. Add potatoes, simmer, covered, about 30 minutes or until lamb is tender. Add eggplants to lamb mixture; simmer, uncovered, 30 minutes. Discard leaves, whole spices and rind before serving; stir in nuts and coconut milk. Serves 6.

- Recipe can be made a day ahead.
- Storage: Covered, in refrigerator.
- Freeze: Suitable; stir in nuts and coconut milk after reheating.
- Microwave: Not suitable.
- Slow cooker: Suitable.
- Pressure cooker: Suitable.
- Conventional oven: Suitable.

IRISH STEW

¼ cup (60ml) vegetable oil
2kg lamb neck chops
1 medium (350g) leek, chopped
3 large (900g) potatoes, chopped
2 medium (240g) carrots, chopped
1 tablespoon chopped fresh thyme
1 litre (4 cups) lamb or chicken stock

Heat half the oil in pan, add chops in batches, cook until lightly browned all over; remove from pan. Heat remaining oil in same pan, add leek, cook, stirring, until just tender. Add potatoes, carrots and thyme, then return chops to pan with stock, simmer, covered, about 1 hour or until chops are tender.
Serves 6 to 8.

■ Recipe can be made a day ahead.
■ Storage: Covered, in refrigerator.
■ Freeze: Suitable.

♣ Microwave: Not suitable.
♣ Slow cooker: Suitable.
♣ Pressure cooker: Suitable.
♣ Conventional oven: Suitable.

LAMB AND BEETROOT WITH PARSNIP PUREE

1 bunch (1.6kg) beetroot
1.5kg diced lamb
plain flour
2 tablespoons olive oil
2 large (400g) onions, sliced
1 clove garlic, crushed
2½ cups (625ml) lamb or beef stock
¾ cup (180ml) port
1 tablespoon chopped fresh sage
1 teaspoon ground black pepper
1 tablespoon chopped fresh parsley

PARSNIP PUREE
6 large (1kg) parsnips, chopped
1 teaspoon seasoned pepper
40g butter
2 tablespoons cream
1 tablespoon chopped fresh parsley

Boil, steam or microwave unpeeled beetroot until just tender; cool. Peel beetroot, cut into wedges. Toss lamb in flour; shake away excess flour. Heat oil in large pan, add lamb in batches, cook, stirring, until browned; drain on absorbent paper. Add onions and garlic to same pan, cook, stirring, until onions are soft. Add stock, port, sage, pepper and lamb to pan, simmer, covered, 40 minutes.

Stir parsley and beetroot into lamb mixture, simmer, uncovered, about 10 minutes or until beetroot is hot. Serve with parsnip puree.
Parsnip Puree: Boil, steam or microwave parsnips until tender; drain. Blend or process parsnips with remaining ingredients until smooth.
Serves 6.

■ Lamb can be made a day ahead; add parsley and beetroot just before serving.
■ Storage: Covered, in refrigerator.
■ Freeze: Not suitable.

♣ Microwave: Beetroot and parsnips suitable.
♣ Slow cooker: Suitable.
♣ Pressure cooker: Suitable.
♣ Conventional oven: Lamb suitable.

LEFT: Irish Stew.
ABOVE: Lamb and Beetroot with Parsnip Puree.

MINTED LAMB RACKS

4 racks (3 cutlets each) of lamb
1½ tablespoons vegetable oil
1 medium (170g) red Spanish onion,
**   finely chopped**
2 sticks celery, finely chopped
1 medium (150g) apple,
**   finely chopped**
¾ cup (180ml) beef stock
1 tablespoon chopped fresh mint
2 teaspoons chopped fresh sage

MARINADE
½ cup (125ml) fruit chutney
½ cup (125ml) dry white wine
2 cloves garlic, crushed
½ teaspoon ground cumin
½ teaspoon ground coriander

Combine lamb and marinade in bowl; mix well. Cover, refrigerate several hours or overnight.

Drain lamb; reserve marinade. Heat half the oil in flameproof casserole dish (1.5 litre/6 cup capacity), add onion, celery and apple, cook, stirring, until onion is soft; remove from dish. Heat remaining oil in same dish, add lamb, cook until browned all over. Return onion mixture to dish, add stock, reserved marinade and herbs, bring to boil. Bake, covered, in moderate oven about 1 hour or until lamb is tender. Cut lamb into cutlets before serving.

Marinade: Combine all ingredients in bowl; mix well.

Serves 4.

■ Recipe best marinated a day ahead.
■ Storage: Covered, in refrigerator.
■ Freeze: Suitable.
♣ Microwave: Not suitable.
♣ Slow cooker: Suitable.
♣ Pressure cooker: Suitable.
♣ Cook-top: Suitable.

ABOVE: Minted Lamb Racks.
RIGHT: Lamb Pot Roast.

Right: Platter and jug from Corso De' Fiori.

LAMB POT ROAST

2 x 1kg boned rolled lamb shoulders
2 cloves garlic, crushed
2 fresh rosemary sprigs
1 teaspoon chopped fresh thyme
1 teaspoon grated orange rind
1 cup (250ml) dry red wine
1 teaspoon olive oil
4 bacon rashers, chopped
1 bunch (370g) spring onions, trimmed
1 tablespoon chicken stock powder
12 baby (480g) new potatoes
2 medium (240g) carrots, halved
2 teaspoons cornflour
1 tablespoon water

Combine lamb, garlic, herbs, rind and wine in bowl; cover, refrigerate several hours or overnight.

Remove lamb from marinade; reserve marinade. Pat lamb dry with absorbent paper, brush with oil. Heat deep flame-proof casserole dish (3 litre/12 cup capacity), add lamb, cook until browned all over; remove from dish. Add bacon and onions to dish, cook, stirring, until onions are lightly browned.

Return lamb to dish, add reserved marinade and stock powder, bake, covered, in moderate oven 45 minutes. Add potatoes and carrots, bake, covered, about 1 hour or until lamb and vegetables are tender. Remove lamb and vegetables from dish.

Discard all but 2 cups (500ml) of the cooking liquid. Blend cornflour with water, add to dish, stir in cooking liquid, stir over heat until mixture boils and thickens. Serve sliced lamb and vegetables with sauce.

Serves 6 to 8.

■ Recipe can be made a day ahead.
■ Storage: Covered, in refrigerator.
■ Freeze: Suitable; thicken with cornflour just before serving.

● Microwave: Not suitable.
● Slow cooker: Suitable.
● Pressure cooker: Suitable.
● Cook-top: Suitable.

BRAISED LAMB SHANKS WITH SUN-DRIED TOMATOES

10 large (3kg) lamb shanks
plain flour
2 tablespoons olive oil
12 baby (300g) onions
½ cup (55g) drained sun-dried
   tomatoes
½ cup (125ml) port
1½ cups (375ml) dry red wine
½ cup (125ml) chicken stock
2 tablespoons chopped fresh parsley

Toss lamb in flour, shake away excess flour. Heat oil in large baking dish, add lamb in batches, cook until browned all over; drain on absorbent paper. Return lamb to dish, add onions, tomatoes, port, wine and stock, cover, bake in moderate oven about 2 hours or until lamb is tender. Remove lamb from dish; keep warm. Simmer pan juices over heat until slightly thickened. Serve lamb with pan juices, sprinkle with parsley. Serves 4 to 6.

■ Recipe best made on day of serving.
■ Storage: Covered, in refrigerator.
■ Freeze: Suitable.

♣ Microwave: Not suitable.
♣ Slow cooker: Suitable.
♣ Pressure cooker: Suitable.
♣ Cook-top: Suitable.

LAMB WITH MUSHROOMS AND POTATOES

8 (1kg) lamb chump chops
plain flour
2 tablespoons vegetable oil
4 bacon rashers, chopped
150g flat mushrooms, quartered
150g button mushrooms
1 clove garlic, crushed
1 cup (250ml) beef stock
1 tablespoon red wine vinegar
12 baby (480g) new potatoes
2 tablespoons chopped fresh parsley

Trim fat from chops. Toss chops in flour; shake away excess flour. Heat half the oil in flameproof casserole dish (3 litre/ 12 cup capacity), add chops in batches, cook until browned; remove from dish. Heat remaining oil in same dish, add bacon, mushrooms and garlic, cook, stirring, 5 minutes. Return chops to dish, add stock, vinegar and potatoes, bring to boil, bake, covered, in moderate oven about 45 minutes or until chops are tender. Serve sprinkled with parsley. Serves 4.

■ Recipe can be made a day ahead.
■ Storage: Covered, in refrigerator.
■ Freeze: Not suitable.

♣ Microwave: Not suitable.
♣ Slow cooker: Suitable.
♣ Pressure cooker: Suitable.
♣ Cook-top: Suitable.

LEFT: Braised Lamb Shanks with Sun-Dried Tomatoes.
RIGHT: Lamb with Mushrooms and Potatoes.

Left: Serving spoons from Morris Home & Garden Wares.

LAMB WITH REDCURRANT AND RED WINE SAUCE

2 tablespoons vegetable oil
1.5kg leg of lamb
4 medium (480g) carrots, chopped
4 medium (500g) parsnips, chopped
6 small (480g) onions, quartered
4 cloves garlic, crushed
3 bacon rashers, chopped
2 tablespoons redcurrant jelly
2 tablespoons tomato paste
1 cup (250ml) dry red wine
1 beef stock cube, crumbled
1 tablespoon chopped fresh thyme

Heat oil in large pan, add lamb, cook until browned all over; remove from pan. Add carrots, parsnips, onions, garlic and bacon to same pan, cook, stirring, until lightly browned.

Add remaining ingredients, bring to boil, return lamb to pan, simmer, covered, about 1¼ hours or until tender. Serve lamb sliced with sauce and vegetables. Serves 4.

■ Recipe can be made a day ahead.
■ Storage: Covered, in refrigerator.
■ Freeze: Suitable.

♣ Microwave: Not suitable.
♣ Slow cooker: Suitable.
♣ Pressure cooker: Suitable.
♣ Conventional oven: Suitable.

ABOVE: Lamb with Redcurrant and Red Wine Sauce.
RIGHT: Lamb Cutlets with Mustard and Lemon.

Above: Platter from Country Floors; wire basket for glasses from Morris Home & Garden Wares.
Right: Plate and tiles from Morris Home & Garden Wares.

LAMB CUTLETS WITH MUSTARD AND LEMON

12 (780g) lamb cutlets
1 tablespoon olive oil
6 cloves garlic, peeled
2 teaspoons chopped fresh rosemary
1 cup (250ml) lamb or beef stock
1 teaspoon grated lemon rind
1 tablespoon soy sauce
2 teaspoons seeded mustard
12 baby (480g) potatoes, quartered
2 tablespoons cornflour
2 tablespoons water

Trim excess fat from lamb. Heat oil in flameproof casserole dish (3 litre/12 cup capacity), add lamb in batches, cook until browned all over. Drain oil from dish. Return lamb and any juices to dish, add garlic, rosemary, stock, rind, sauce and mustard. Bake, covered, in moderate oven about 1½ hours or until lamb is tender. Stir potatoes and blended cornflour and water into dish. Bake, uncovered, in moderate oven about 15 minutes or until potatoes are tender. Serves 4 to 6.

■ Recipe can be made a day ahead.
■ Storage: Covered, in refrigerator.
■ Freeze: Suitable; thicken with cornflour just before serving.
● Microwave: Not suitable.
● Slow cooker: Suitable.
● Pressure cooker: Suitable.
● Cook-top: Suitable.

KUMARA-TOPPED LAMB

1.5kg diced lamb
plain flour
¼ cup (60ml) vegetable oil
2 medium (700g) leeks, sliced
2 medium (600g) eggplants, chopped
1 clove garlic, crushed
¾ cup (180ml) beef stock
½ cup (125ml) tomato puree
2 teaspoons chopped fresh thyme

KUMARA TOPPING
2 large (1kg) kumara, chopped
40g butter
⅓ cup (80ml) sour cream
⅓ cup (25g) grated parmesan
    cheese
1 tablespoon chopped fresh parsley

Toss lamb in flour; shake away excess flour. Heat 2 tablespoons of the oil in flameproof casserole dish (2.5 litre/10 cup capacity), add lamb in batches, cook, stirring, until browned; remove from dish. Heat remaining oil in same dish, add leeks, eggplants and garlic, cook, stirring, 5 minutes. Return lamb to dish, add stock, puree and thyme, simmer, covered, about 40 minutes, stirring occasionally, or until lamb is tender.

Spoon kumara topping into piping bag fitted with large star tube, pipe topping over lamb mixture. Bake, uncovered, in moderately hot oven about 30 minutes or until lightly browned.

Kumara Topping: Boil, steam or microwave kumara until tender; drain. Process kumara with remaining ingredients until mixture is smooth.

Serves 6 to 8.

- ■ Recipe can be made a day ahead.
- ■ Storage: Covered, in refrigerator.
- ■ Freeze: Lamb suitable.
- ♣ Microwave: Kumara suitable.
- ♣ Slow cooker: Lamb suitable.
- ♣ Pressure cooker: Lamb suitable.
- ♣ Conventional oven: Suitable.

RIGHT: Minted Lamb with Cider and Vegetables.
BELOW: Kumara-Topped Lamb.

Right: China from Waterford Wedgwood.
Below: Plates from Villeroy & Boch.

MINTED LAMB WITH CIDER AND VEGETABLES

¼ cup (60ml) vegetable oil
12 baby (300g) onions
1kg diced lamb
plain flour
1 cup (250ml) sweet alcoholic cider
2½ cups (625ml) water
2 small lamb or beef stock cubes
1 bunch (20) baby carrots
1 cup (125g) frozen peas
⅓ cup chopped fresh mint

Heat 1 tablespoon of the oil in large pan, add onions, cook, stirring, until onions are browned; remove from pan. Toss lamb in flour; shake away excess flour. Heat remaining oil in same pan, add lamb in batches, cook, stirring, until browned; drain on absorbent paper. Return lamb to pan, add cider, water and crumbled stock cubes, simmer, covered, 1 hour. Add onions and carrots to lamb mixture, simmer, covered, 45 minutes or until lamb is tender, stirring occasionally. Add peas, simmer, uncovered, about 5 minutes or until peas are tender; stir in mint.

Serves 6.

■ Recipe can be made a day ahead.
■ Storage: Covered, in refrigerator.
■ Freeze: Suitable; add peas and mint just before serving.

● Microwave: Not suitable.
● Slow cooker: Suitable.
● Pressure cooker: Suitable.
● Conventional oven: Suitable.

LANCASHIRE HOT POT

8 (1kg) lamb neck chops
3 medium (450g) onions, sliced
3 large (900g) potatoes, sliced
4 bacon rashers, chopped
1¾ cups (430ml) beef stock
30g butter, chopped

Trim fat from chops, place chops in ovenproof casserole dish (3 litre/12 cup capacity). Top with a layer of onions, potatoes and bacon. Repeat layering, ending with potatoes. Pour over stock, top with butter.

Bake, covered, in moderately slow oven 2 hours. Remove cover, bake about 1 hour or until chops are tender. Serves 4 to 6.

■ Recipe best made just before serving.
■ Freeze: Suitable.

🍲 Microwave: Not suitable.
🍲 Slow cooker: Suitable.
🍲 Pressure cooker: Suitable.
🍲 Cook-top: Suitable.

SPICED APRICOT AND LAMB TAGINE

¼ cup (60ml) olive oil
1kg diced lamb
2 cloves garlic, crushed
1 large (200g) onion, chopped
¼ teaspoon ground cinnamon
½ teaspoon ground cumin
½ teaspoon ground ginger
½ teaspoon ground turmeric
3 cups (750ml) water
1 cinnamon stick
2 strips lemon rind
1½ tablespoons honey
1 cup (150g) dried apricots
½ cup (80g) blanched almonds, toasted
2 tablespoons chopped fresh coriander
1 tablespoon sesame seeds, toasted

Heat oil in pan, add lamb in batches, cook, stirring, until browned; remove from pan. Add garlic, onion and ground spices to same pan, cook, stirring, until onion is soft. Stir in water, cinnamon stick and rind. Return lamb to pan, simmer, covered, about 1½ hours or until lamb is tender.

Add honey, apricots and nuts to lamb mixture, simmer, uncovered, 10 minutes or until apricots are tender. Discard cinnamon stick and rind; stir in coriander. Serve sprinkled with sesame seeds. Serves 4 to 6.

■ Recipe can be made a day ahead.
■ Storage: Covered, in refrigerator.
■ Freeze: Suitable without coriander.

🍲 Microwave: Not suitable.
🍲 Slow cooker: Suitable.
🍲 Pressure cooker: Suitable.
🍲 Conventional oven: Suitable.

ABOVE: Spiced Apricot and Lamb Tagine.
RIGHT: Lancashire Hot Pot.

Right: Tiles from Country Floors.

Pork & Veal

These delicious dishes show a truly up-to-date approach to traditional styles of cooking. Instead of veal you could substitute yearling (year old beef), but this might need more cooking to tenderise. Most recipes are suitable for a slow cooker or pressure cooker; any thickening with flour is done just before serving.

BACON AND VEGETABLES WITH SCONE TOPPING

40g butter
3 bacon rashers, chopped
2 medium (400g) potatoes, chopped
1 medium (150g) onion, chopped
3 (180g) finger eggplants, chopped
1/3 cup (80ml) dry red wine
1 1/2 cups (375ml) chicken stock
1 small (150g) swede, chopped
300g pumpkin, chopped
1 medium (120g) carrot, chopped
1/2 cup (125ml) tomato puree
1 large (150g) zucchini, chopped
150g button mushrooms, halved
1 tablespoon chopped fresh basil

CHEESE AND BACON SCONES
1 small (80g) onion, finely chopped
1 bacon rasher, finely chopped
2 cups (300g) self-raising flour
1 teaspoon dry mustard
50g butter, chopped
1/2 cup (40g) grated parmesan cheese
1 tablespoon chopped fresh parsley
2/3 cup (160ml) milk, approximately

Heat butter in flameproof casserole dish (2 litre/ 8 cup capacity), add bacon, potatoes and onion, cook, stirring, until onion is soft. Add eggplants, cook, stirring, 3 minutes. Add wine, simmer, uncovered, until most of the liquid has evaporated. Add stock, swede, pumpkin, carrot and puree, simmer, uncovered, 10 minutes. Add zucchini, mushrooms and basil, simmer, covered, about 15 minutes or until vegetables are tender. Top with cheese and bacon scones, brush scones with a little milk or water. Bake in hot oven about 15 minutes or until scones are cooked through.

Cheese and Bacon Scones: Cook onion and bacon in pan, stirring, until onion is soft; drain on absorbent paper, cool. Sift flour and mustard into bowl, rub in butter, stir in onion mixture, cheese and parsley. Stir in enough milk to mix to a soft, sticky dough. Turn dough onto floured surface, knead lightly until smooth, press until about 2cm thick, cut into 4cm rounds.
Serves 6.

- Recipe best made just before serving.
- Freeze: Not suitable.

- Microwave: Not suitable.
- Slow cooker: Not suitable.
- Pressure cooker: Not suitable.
- Conventional oven: Vegetable mixture not suitable.

RIGHT: Bacon and Vegetables with Scone Topping.

China from Waterford Wedgwood.

VEAL WITH EGGPLANT, OLIVES AND CAPERS

1.5kg diced veal
plain flour
2 tablespoons olive oil
1 bunch (10) spring onions, trimmed, halved
4 cloves garlic, crushed
1 tablespoon drained capers, finely chopped
1 large (500g) eggplant, chopped
10 medium (1.3kg) tomatoes, chopped
¼ cup (60ml) tomato paste
1 cup (250ml) dry white wine
2 teaspoons chopped fresh thyme
2 bay leaves
¼ cup (40g) seedless black olives
2 tablespoons pine nuts, toasted
2 tablespoons chopped fresh mint

Toss veal in flour, shake away excess flour. Heat oil in flameproof casserole dish (3 litre/12 cup capacity), add veal in batches, cook until browned; remove from dish. Add onions, garlic, capers and eggplant to dish, cook, stirring, 5 minutes. Add veal, then stir in tomatoes, paste, wine, thyme and bay leaves. Bake, covered, in moderate oven about 2 hours or until veal is tender. Discard bay leaves; serve topped with olives, nuts and mint.
Serves 6.

■ Recipe can be made a day ahead.
■ Storage: Covered, in refrigerator.
■ Freeze: Suitable.

♣ Microwave: Not suitable.
♣ Slow cooker: Suitable.
♣ Pressure cooker: Suitable.
♣ Cook-top: Suitable.

VEAL CHOPS WITH THYME AND VEGETABLES

12 small (1.4kg) veal chops
¼ cup (35g) plain flour
1 tablespoon Cajun seasoning
2 tablespoons vegetable oil
2 cups (500ml) chicken stock
½ cup (125ml) dry white wine
½ bunch (10) baby carrots
1 bunch (10) spring onions, trimmed
2 fresh corn cobs, sliced
2 teaspoons chopped fresh thyme
2 bay leaves
150g green beans, halved
1 tablespoon chopped fresh parsley

Toss chops in combined flour and Cajun seasoning; shake away excess flour mixture, reserve excess flour mixture. Heat oil in pan, add chops in batches, cook until browned all over; remove from pan. Stir reserved flour mixture into same pan, stir over heat until bubbling. Remove from heat, gradually stir in stock and wine, stir over heat until sauce boils and thickens.

Return chops to pan. Stir in carrots, onions, corn, thyme and bay leaves, simmer, covered, 20 minutes, stirring occasionally. Stir in beans, simmer, covered, about 15 minutes or until chops and vegetables are tender. Discard bay leaves; stir in parsley.
Serves 6.

■ Recipe can be made a day ahead.
▨ Storage: Covered, in refrigerator.
■ Freeze: Suitable.

♣ Microwave: Not suitable.
♣ Slow cooker: Suitable.
♣ Pressure cooker: Suitable.
♣ Conventional oven: Suitable.

ABOVE: Veal with Eggplant, Olives and Capers.
RIGHT: Veal Chops with Thyme and Vegetables.

Right: Platter from Country Floors.

VEAL WITH SPINACH AND MUSHROOMS

1 tablespoon olive oil
1.5kg diced veal
2 medium (700g) leeks, sliced
2 teaspoons chopped fresh thyme
½ cup (125ml) dry white wine
2 small chicken stock cubes
425g can tomatoes
500g button mushrooms
1 medium (200g) red pepper,
    chopped
1 bunch (500g) English spinach,
    roughly chopped
¼ cup shredded fresh basil

Heat oil in large pan, add veal in batches, cook, stirring, until browned. Return veal to pan with leeks and thyme, cook, stirring, until leeks are soft. Stir in wine, crumbled stock cubes, undrained crushed tomatoes, mushrooms and pepper, simmer, covered, about 1½ hours or until veal is very tender. Just before serving, stir in spinach and basil. Serve with rice, if desired.

Serves 6.

■ Recipe can be made a day ahead.
■ Storage: Covered, in refrigerator.
■ Freeze: Suitable.

♣ Microwave: Not suitable.
♣ Slow cooker: Suitable.
♣ Pressure cooker: Suitable.
♣ Conventional oven: Suitable.

RIGHT: Veal and Peppers with Polenta Cakes.
BELOW: Veal with Spinach and Mushrooms.

Right: Casserole dish, stand and cutlery

VEAL AND PEPPERS WITH POLENTA CAKES

1.5kg diced veal
plain flour
2 tablespoons olive oil
3 cloves garlic, crushed
1½ cups (375ml) beef stock
425g can tomatoes
1½ tablespoons chopped
    fresh oregano
2 tablespoons chopped fresh parsley
1 small (150g) red pepper, sliced
1 small (150g) green pepper, sliced
1 small (150g) yellow pepper, sliced

POLENTA CAKES
¾ cup (105g) self-raising flour
1 tablespoon polenta
30g butter, chopped
1 teaspoon chopped fresh rosemary
½ cup (60g) grated tasty
cheddar cheese
2 teaspoons grated parmesan
cheese
¼ cup (60ml) milk, approximately

Toss veal in flour, shake away excess flour. Heat oil in flameproof casserole dish (2.5 litre/10 cup capacity), add veal and garlic in batches, cook, stirring, until browned; remove from dish. Add stock and undrained crushed tomatoes to same dish, bring to boil, add veal and herbs, bake, covered, in moderate oven 1 hour. Stir in peppers, top with polenta cakes, bake, uncovered, about 30 minutes or until polenta cakes are browned.

Polenta Cakes: Sift flour into bowl, add polenta, rub in butter; add rosemary and cheeses. Stir in enough milk to form a soft dough. Knead dough on floured surface until smooth, press mixture to 1cm thickness; cut into 3cm rounds.

Serves 6.

- Veal mixture can be made a day ahead. Polenta cakes best made just before serving.
- Storage: Covered, in refrigerator.
- Freeze: Veal suitable.
- Microwave: Not suitable.
- Slow cooker: Veal suitable.
- Pressure cooker: Veal suitable.
- Cook-top: Veal suitable.

BRAISED VEAL ROLLS WITH PASTA AND OLIVES

Any small soup pasta can be used.

4 large (1.4kg) red peppers
1/2 bunch (250g) English spinach
8 (900g) veal steaks
1/4 cup (60ml) olive oil
2 medium (300g) onions,
  finely chopped
2 cloves garlic, crushed
425g can tomato puree
1/3 cup (80ml) dry red wine
2 teaspoons sugar
1/2 cup (100g) stellettine pasta
3/4 cup (120g) seedless black olives
2 tablespoons shredded fresh basil

Quarter peppers, remove seeds and membranes. Grill peppers, skin side up, until skin blisters and blackens. Peel away skin. Place spinach leaves over each veal steak, top with peppers. Roll veal tightly, secure with toothpicks.

Heat 2 tablespoons of the oil in pan, add veal in batches, cook until browned all over; drain on absorbent paper. Heat remaining oil in same pan, add onions and garlic, cook, stirring, until onions are soft. Add puree, wine, sugar and veal, simmer, covered, 15 minutes. Add pasta and olives, simmer, covered, about 7 minutes or until pasta is tender. Serve veal sliced with sauce, sprinkled with basil. Serves 6 to 8.

■ Recipe best made close to serving.
■ Freeze: Not suitable.

♣ Microwave: Not suitable.
♣ Slow cooker: Not suitable.
♣ Pressure cooker: Not suitable.
♣ Conventional oven: Suitable.

PORK WITH CHESTNUTS, PORT AND FIGS

We used a dish with a base measuring 23cm, so the pork was covered with liquid during cooking.

1/3 cup (80ml) port
1/2 cup (95g) chopped dried figs
1.8kg pork neck
1 tablespoon vegetable oil
2 1/2 cups (625ml) beef stock
425g can chestnuts, rinsed, drained
1 tablespoon seeded mustard
2 tablespoons chopped fresh
  parsley

Combine port and figs in small bowl, cover, stand 1 hour. Secure pork with string at 2cm intervals, to make an even shape. Heat oil in flameproof casserole dish (5 litre/20 cup capacity), add pork, cook, turning, until browned all over. Add stock and undrained fig mixture, simmer, covered, turning occasionally, about 2 hours or until pork is tender. Stir in chestnuts and mustard, cook, uncovered, until heated through. Serve sprinkled with parsley.
Serves 8.

■ Recipe can be made a day ahead.
■ Storage: Covered, in refrigerator.
■ Freeze: Suitable.

♣ Microwave: Not suitable.
♣ Slow cooker: Suitable.
♣ Pressure cooker: Suitable.
♣ Conventional oven: Suitable.

LEFT: Braised Veal Rolls with Pasta and Olives.
ABOVE: Pork with Chestnuts, Port and Figs.

Left: Glass from Home & Garden on the Mall.

HUNGARIAN-STYLE GOULASH

1kg forequarter veal, chopped
1 tablespoon paprika
2 tablespoons plain flour
2 teaspoons caraway seeds
1 tablespoon vegetable oil
20g butter
1 medium (150g) onion, chopped
1 cup (250ml) beef stock
2 x 425g cans tomatoes
1 tablespoon tomato paste
3 medium (600g) potatoes, chopped
2 teaspoons chopped fresh oregano

Toss veal in combined paprika, flour and seeds; shake away excess flour mixture. Heat oil and butter in pan, add veal in batches, cook, stirring, until browned; remove from pan. Add onion to same pan, cook, stirring, until soft. Return veal to pan with stock, undrained crushed tomatoes and paste, simmer, covered, 30 minutes. Add potatoes, simmer, covered, about 30 minutes or until veal and potatoes are tender. Remove cover, simmer about 5 minutes or until slightly thickened; stir in oregano.
Serves 6.

■ Recipe can be made a day ahead.
■ Storage: Covered, in refrigerator.
■ Freeze: Suitable.

♣ Microwave: Not suitable.
♣ Slow cooker: Suitable.
♣ Pressure cooker: Suitable.
♣ Conventional oven: Suitable.

LEFT: Hungarian-Style Goulash.
ABOVE: Veal Pot Roast with Olives and Baby Onions.
Above: Platter from Waterford Wedgwood; serving fork and white china mould from The Bay Tree Kitchen Shop.

VEAL POT ROAST WITH OLIVES AND BABY ONIONS

2 tablespoons olive oil
1.5kg rolled shoulder of veal
8 baby (200g) onions
3 cloves garlic, crushed
1 medium (200g) red pepper, sliced
2 tablespoons tomato paste
425g can tomatoes
¼ cup chopped fresh basil
½ cup (125ml) port
½ cup (125ml) chicken stock
⅓ cup (50g) seedless green olives

Heat oil in large pan, add veal, cook until browned all over; remove from pan. Add onions and garlic to same pan, cook, stirring, until onions are lightly browned. Add pepper, paste and undrained crushed tomatoes, cook, stirring, 2 minutes. Return veal to pan, add basil, port and stock, simmer, covered, about 1¼ hours or until veal is tender. Just before serving, add olives, simmer, covered, 5 minutes. Serve veal sliced with tomato mixture.
Serves 6 to 8.

- Recipe can be made a day ahead.
- Storage: Covered, in refrigerator.
- Freeze: Suitable.
- Microwave: Not suitable.
- Slow cooker: Suitable.
- Pressure cooker: Suitable.
- Conventional oven: Suitable.

APPLES, PORK AND PRUNES

2 tablespoons vegetable oil
2 small (400g) leeks, sliced
4 (1.75kg) forequarter pork chops
plain flour
1 litre (4 cups) chicken stock
½ cup (100g) long-grain rice
4 medium (600g) apples,
    thickly sliced
1 cup (170g) seedless prunes
2 tablespoons chopped fresh sage

Heat half the oil in flameproof casserole dish (2.5 litre/10 cup capacity), add leeks, cook, stirring, until soft; remove from dish. Trim fat and bone from chops; cut pork into 5cm pieces. Toss pork in flour, shake away excess flour. Heat remaining oil in same dish, add pork, cook, stirring, until browned. Add leeks and stock to dish, bake, covered, in moderate oven 45 minutes. Remove dish from oven, skim off any fat. Stir in rice, apples, prunes and half the sage, cook, covered, about 30 minutes or until pork is tender. Serve sprinkled with remaining sage.

Serves 4 to 6.

■ Recipe can be made a day ahead.
■ Storage: Covered, in refrigerator.
■ Freeze: Suitable.
♣ Microwave: Not suitable.
♣ Slow cooker: Suitable.
♣ Pressure cooker: Suitable.
♣ Cook-top: Suitable.

ABOVE: Apples, Pork and Prunes.
RIGHT: Ragout of Veal and Mushrooms.

Above: China from Waterford Wedgwood.
Right: China from Johnson Brothers for Waterford Wedgewood

RAGOUT OF VEAL AND MUSHROOMS

1.5kg diced veal
plain flour
20g butter
1½ tablespoons olive oil
1 medium (350g) leek, chopped
2 cloves garlic, crushed
1 cup (250ml) dry white wine
1 litre (4 cups) water
2 tablespoons tomato paste
1 teaspoon ground black pepper
300g button mushrooms, sliced
⅓ cup (80ml) cream

Toss veal in flour; shake away excess flour. Heat butter and oil in pan, add veal in batches, cook until lightly browned; drain on absorbent paper. Add leek and garlic to same pan, cook, covered, until leek is soft. Add wine, cook, stirring, until liquid is reduced by half. Return veal to pan, add water, paste and pepper, simmer, covered, 30 minutes. Add mushrooms, simmer, uncovered, about 20 minutes or until liquid has thickened slightly. Stir in cream just before serving.
Serves 6 to 8.

■ Recipe can be made a day ahead.
■ Storage: Covered, in refrigerator.
■ Freeze: Suitable.

♣ Microwave: Not suitable.
♣ Slow cooker: Suitable.
♣ Pressure cooker: Suitable.
♣ Conventional oven: Suitable.

BRAISED NUT OF VEAL WITH GARLIC MUSHROOMS

2 tablespoons olive oil
2 (1.2kg) nuts of veal
12 (120g) spring onions, trimmed
3 cloves garlic, crushed
500g button mushrooms
¼ cup (60ml) dry red wine
1 cup (250ml) tomato puree
1 cup (250ml) chicken stock
1 teaspoon chopped fresh thyme
2 bay leaves
1½ tablespoons cornflour
¼ cup (60ml) water

Heat oil in flameproof casserole dish (2.5 litre/10 cup capacity), add veal, cook until browned all over; remove from dish. Add onions, garlic and mushrooms to same dish, cook, stirring, 3 minutes. Add veal, wine, puree, stock, thyme and bay leaves, bake, covered, in moderate oven about 1 hour or until veal is tender. Remove veal and vegetables from dish. Stir in blended cornflour and water, stir over heat until mixture boils and thickens; remove bay leaves. Serve veal sliced with vegetables and sauce, sprinkle with chopped parsley, if desired.

Serves 6.

- Recipe best made just before serving.
- Freeze: Not suitable.
- Microwave: Not suitable.
- Slow cooker: Suitable.
- Pressure cooker: Suitable.
- Cook-top: Suitable.

CREAMY VEAL, MUSHROOMS AND BROAD BEANS

2 tablespoons olive oil
1.5kg veal loin chops
2 large (400g) onions, sliced
4 cloves garlic, crushed
250g button mushrooms, quartered
2 tablespoons plain flour
1 cup (250ml) chicken stock
1 cup (250ml) dry white wine
2 teaspoons chopped fresh thyme
1 cup (150g) frozen broad beans, thawed, peeled
⅓ cup (80ml) sour cream

Heat oil in flameproof casserole dish (2.5 litre/10 cup capacity), add veal in batches, cook until browned all over; remove from dish. Add onions, garlic and mushrooms to dish, cook, stirring, until onions are soft. Sprinkle flour over onion mixture, cook, stirring, 3 minutes, gradually stir in stock, wine and thyme. Add veal, bake, covered, in moderate oven about 1½ hours or until veal is tender. Just before serving, stir in beans and sour cream, bake about 10 minutes or until hot.

Serves 4 to 6.

- Recipe can be made a day ahead.
- Storage: Covered, in refrigerator.
- Freeze: Not suitable.
- Microwave: Not suitable.
- Slow cooker: Suitable.
- Pressure cooker: Suitable.
- Cook-top: Suitable.

LEFT: Braised Nut of Veal with Garlic Mushrooms.
BELOW: Creamy Veal, Mushrooms and Broad Beans.

Left: China from Villeroy & Boch. Below: Casserole dish from The Bay Tree Kitchen Shop; green egg basket from Emile Henry.

HERBED VEAL IN LEMON CREAM SAUCE

We used French Gourmet Herbs consisting of parsley flakes, chervil, tarragon leaves and chives.

70g butter
2 medium (300g) onions, sliced
2 cloves garlic, crushed
¼ cup (35g) plain flour
2 teaspoons French-style dried mixed herbs
1.25kg diced veal
3 cups (750ml) chicken stock
2 medium (240g) carrots, sliced
125g button mushrooms, halved
2 tablespoons lemon juice
¼ cup (60ml) creme fraiche
2 tablespoons chopped fresh parsley

Heat butter in flameproof casserole dish (4.5 litre/18 cup capacity), add onions, cook, stirring, until soft. Add garlic, flour and herbs, cook, stirring, until bubbling. Add veal, stir until lightly browned. Add stock and carrots. Bake, covered, in moderately slow oven about 1½ hours or until veal is tender. Stir in mushrooms, bake, covered, 30 minutes. Stir in juice, creme fraiche and half the parsley. Serve veal sprinkled with remaining parsley. Serves 6.

■ Recipe can be made a day ahead.
■ Storage: Covered, in refrigerator.
■ Freeze: Suitable; stir in mushrooms when reheating.

♣ Microwave: Not suitable.
♣ Slow cooker: Suitable.
♣ Pressure cooker: Suitable.
♣ Cook-top: Suitable.

ABOVE: Herbed Veal in Lemon Cream Sauce.
RIGHT: Veal and Prosciutto Roll with Caramelised Onions.

Above: Tablecloth from Pacific East India Company. Right: Dish from Waterford Wedgwood.

VEAL AND PROSCIUTTO ROLL WITH CARAMELISED ONIONS

2 cloves garlic, crushed
2 teaspoons chopped fresh sage
2 teaspoons chopped fresh thyme
1 teaspoon ground black pepper
1.5kg shoulder of veal, boned
3 slices (45g) prosciutto
2 tablespoons olive oil
½ cup (125ml) dry red wine
1½ cups (375ml) beef stock

CARAMELISED ONIONS
1 tablespoon olive oil
30g butter
4 large (800g) onions, sliced
1 teaspoon chopped fresh sage
1 cup (160g) seedless black olives

Combine garlic, herbs and pepper in small bowl; mix well. Rub garlic mixture all over cut side of veal, top with prosciutto, roll up firmly, secure with string at 2cm intervals. Heat oil in baking dish, add veal to dish, cook until browned all over. Pour over wine and stock, bake, covered, in moderately hot oven about 1¼ hours or until veal is tender. Remove veal from dish, cover, keep warm. Simmer pan juices over heat until reduced by half. Serve veal with pan juices and caramelised onions.

Caramelised Onions: Heat oil and butter in pan, add onions and sage, cook, stirring, over low heat about 20 minutes or until browned and caramelised. Add olives, stir until hot.

Serves 6.

■ Veal can be prepared a day ahead. Caramelised onions best cooked just before serving.
■ Storage: Covered, in refrigerator.
■ Freeze: Not suitable.
● Microwave: Not suitable.
● Slow cooker: Veal and prosciutto roll suitable.
● Pressure cooker: Veal and prosciutto roll suitable.
● Cook-top: Suitable.

VEAL CUTLETS WITH BUTTER BEANS AND COUSCOUS

8 (1.4kg) veal cutlets
1/4 cup (35g) plain flour
2 teaspoons paprika
2 tablespoons olive oil
1 medium (170g) red Spanish onion, sliced
2 cloves garlic, crushed
3/4 cup (180ml) beef stock
425g can tomatoes
1/3 cup (35g) drained sun-dried tomatoes
1 tablespoon chopped fresh oregano
310g can butter beans, rinsed, drained

COUSCOUS
1 1/4 cups (310ml) water
1 1/2 cups (300g) couscous
40g butter
1 tablespoon chopped fresh parsley

Toss cutlets in combined flour and paprika; shake away excess flour mixture. Heat half the oil in flameproof casserole dish (2.5 litre/10 cup capacity), add cutlets in batches, cook until browned; remove from dish. Heat remaining oil in same dish, add onion and garlic, cook, stirring, until onion is soft. Return cutlets to dish, add stock, undrained crushed canned tomatoes, sun-dried tomatoes and oregano. Bring to boil, bake, covered, in moderate oven 45 minutes. Stir in beans, bake, covered, 15 minutes. Serve cutlets with sauce and couscous.

Couscous: Bring water to boil in pan, stir in couscous and butter, remove from heat, stand, covered, about 5 minutes or until water is absorbed, stir in parsley. Serves 4 to 6.

- Veal can be made a day ahead. Couscous best made just before serving.
- Storage: Covered, in refrigerator.
- Freeze: Veal suitable.
- Microwave: Couscous suitable.
- Slow cooker: Veal suitable.
- Pressure cooker: Veal suitable.
- Cook-top: Veal suitable.

RIGHT: Pork with Beans 'n' Beer.
BELOW: Veal Cutlets with Butter Beans and Couscous.

Below: China from Villeroy & Boch.

PORK WITH BEANS 'N' BEER

We used a dish with a base measuring 23cm, so the pork was covered with liquid during cooking. Any small white dried bean can be used.

3 cloves garlic, crushed
½ teaspoon freshly ground
    black pepper
1.8kg pork neck
1 tablespoon olive oil
3 bacon rashers, finely chopped
2 medium (300g) onions,
    thinly sliced
2 teaspoons caraway seeds
375ml can beer
1 cup (200g) dried haricot beans
2 cups (500ml) chicken stock
¼ small (300g) white cabbage,
    finely shredded
2 teaspoons fresh thyme leaves

Rub combined garlic and pepper all over pork. Secure pork with string at 2cm intervals to make an even shape. Heat oil in large flameproof casserole dish (5 litre/20 cup capacity), add pork, cook, turning, until browned all over; remove from dish. Add bacon, onions and seeds to same dish, cook, stirring, until onions are soft and bacon lightly browned.

Return pork to dish, add beer, beans and stock, simmer, covered, about 2 hours or until beans and pork are tender. Remove pork from dish. Just before serving, add cabbage, cook, stirring, until just wilted. Serve with sliced pork, sprinkled with thyme.
Serves 8.

■ Recipe can be made a day ahead.
■ Storage: Covered, in refrigerator.
■ Freeze: Suitable.
♣ Microwave: Not suitable.
♣ Slow cooker: Suitable.
♣ Pressure cooker: Suitable.
♣ Conventional oven: Suitable.

OSSO BUCCO

12 (1.5kg) osso bucco
plain flour
2 tablespoons olive oil
2 medium (300g) onions, sliced
4 cloves garlic, crushed
2 x 425g cans tomatoes
½ cup (125ml) dry white wine
1 cup (250ml) beef stock
1 bay leaf
1 tablespoon chopped fresh thyme
1 tablespoon chopped fresh oregano
2 tablespoons chopped fresh parsley

Toss veal in flour; shake away excess flour. Heat oil in pan, add veal in batches, cook until browned all over; drain on absorbent paper. Add onions and garlic to same pan, cook, stirring, until onions are soft. Return veal to pan, add undrained crushed tomatoes, wine, stock, bay leaf, thyme and oregano. Simmer, covered, 1½ hours, stirring occasionally. Remove cover, simmer about 1 hour or until veal is very tender. Discard bay leaf; serve osso bucco sprinkled with parsley.

Serves 4 to 6.

- ■ Recipe can be made a day ahead.
- ■ Storage: Covered, in refrigerator.
- ■ Freeze: Suitable.
- ● Microwave: Not suitable.
- ● Slow cooker: Suitable.
- ● Pressure cooker: Suitable.
- ● Conventional oven: Suitable.

VEAL FRICASSEE

80g butter
1.5kg diced veal
2 large (400g) onions, sliced
½ cup (75g) plain flour
¼ cup (60ml) dry white wine
3 cups (750ml) chicken stock
1 teaspoon cracked black pepper
1 tablespoon chopped fresh parsley
2 teaspoons chopped fresh thyme
3 egg yolks
½ cup (125ml) cream
¼ teaspoon ground nutmeg
2 teaspoons lemon juice

Heat butter in pan, add veal and onions, cook, covered, until onions are soft. Stir in flour, cook, stirring, 3 minutes. Stir in wine, stock, pepper and herbs, simmer, covered, about 45 minutes or until veal is tender. Just before serving, stir in combined egg yolks, cream, nutmeg and juice; stir until hot.
Serves 6.

- ■ Recipe can be prepared a day ahead.
- ■ Storage: Covered, in refrigerator.
- ■ Freeze: Suitable.
- ● Microwave: Not suitable.
- ● Slow cooker: Suitable.
- ● Pressure cooker: Suitable.
- ● Conventional oven: Suitable.

LEFT: Osso Bucco.
ABOVE: Veal Fricassee.

Above: Casserole dish from Emile Henry; jug from Home & Garden on the Mall.

Seafood

You will savour every delicious mouthful of seafood in our wonderful sauces. Seafood should either be cooked quickly for a short time, or gently for a long time; both will result in tender seafood. Follow suggested cooking times carefully; incorrect cooking times will result in tough seafood. If cooking recipes in a microwave oven, be particularly careful as it is very easy to overcook seafood when using this method.

MIXED SEAFOOD COCONUT CURRY

200g small mussels
300g uncooked medium prawns
150g squid hood
2 teaspoons vegetable oil
1 medium (150g) onion, sliced
2 cloves garlic, crushed
1 teaspoon grated fresh ginger
1 teaspoon sambal oelek
1/4 teaspoon belacan
1 tablespoon mild curry powder
1/2 teaspoon ground turmeric
2 3/4 cups (680ml) coconut milk
1/4 cup (60ml) water
1 tablespoon tamarind sauce
150g green beans, halved
1kg boneless white fish fillets, chopped
2 medium (260g) tomatoes, chopped
2 teaspoons chopped fresh coriander

Scrub mussels, remove beards. Shell and devein prawns, leaving tails intact. Cut shallow diagonal slashes on inside surface of squid; cut into 3cm pieces. Heat oil in pan, add onion, garlic, ginger, sambal oelek, belacan, curry powder and turmeric, cook, stirring, until fragrant. Stir in coconut milk, water, tamarind and beans, bring to boil. Add all seafood, simmer, uncovered, about 5 minutes or until seafood is tender. Stir in tomatoes and coriander, stir until heated through.
Serves 4.

- Recipe best made just before serving.
- Freeze: Not suitable.
- Microwave: Suitable.
- Slow cooker: Not suitable.
- Pressure cooker: Not suitable.
- Conventional oven: Not suitable.

RIGHT: Mixed Seafood Coconut Curry.

OCTOPUS AND SQUID CASSEROLE

1kg baby octopus
500g squid hoods
1 tablespoon olive oil
2 cloves garlic, crushed
½ teaspoon sambal oelek
20 baby (500g) onions
1 teaspoon chopped fresh thyme
1 teaspoon chopped fresh oregano
2 teaspoons grated fresh ginger
1 teaspoon grated lime rind
2 x 425g cans tomatoes
1 teaspoon sugar
½ cup (80g) seedless black olives

Discard heads and beaks from octopus; cut octopus in half. Cut squid hoods into 2cm rings. Heat oil in large pan, add garlic, sambal oelek, onions, herbs, ginger and rind, cook, stirring, 2 minutes. Add seafood, undrained crushed tomatoes and sugar, simmer, covered, 30 minutes. Remove cover, simmer about 45 minutes or until seafood is tender and sauce thickened slightly. Stir in olives.

Serves 6.

■ Recipe can be made a day ahead.
■ Storage: Covered, in refrigerator.
■ Freeze: Suitable.

● Microwave: Not suitable.
● Slow cooker: Suitable.
● Pressure cooker: Suitable.
● Conventional oven: Suitable.

FISH KORMA CURRY

30g ghee
2 medium (300g) onions, chopped
500g white sweet potato, chopped
⅓ cup (80ml) korma curry paste
1 cup (250ml) cream
1 cup (250ml) water
1.2kg firm white fish fillets, roughly chopped
1 tablespoon chopped fresh coriander
250g green beans, halved
250g cherry tomatoes

Heat ghee in large pan, add onions, cook, stirring, until onions are just tender. Add sweet potato and paste, cook, stirring, 3 minutes. Add cream and water, simmer, covered, 30 minutes. Add fish, coriander, beans and tomatoes, stir gently, simmer, covered, about 10 minutes or until fish is tender.

Serves 6.

■ Recipe best made close to serving.
■ Freeze: Not suitable.
● Microwave: Suitable.
● Slow cooker: Not suitable.
● Pressure cooker: Not suitable.
● Conventional oven: Not suitable.

LEFT: Octopus and Squid Casserole.
BELOW: Fish Korma Curry.

Left: Plate and serviette from Accoutrement.
Below: Setting from Morris Home & Garden Wares.

QUICK LEMON GRASS AND COCONUT FISH STEW

250g dried noodles
8 Chinese dried mushrooms
1 tablespoon vegetable oil
2 teaspoons grated fresh ginger
2 tablespoons chopped fresh lemon grass
½ teaspoon five spice powder
1 teaspoon ground turmeric
1 teaspoon sambal oelek
400ml can coconut cream
2 chicken stock cubes
¼ cup (60ml) water
1kg boneless white fish fillets, roughly chopped
1 bunch (400g) bok choy, chopped
4 green shallots, chopped

Add noodles to large pan of boiling water, boil, uncovered, until just tender; drain. Place mushrooms in heatproof bowl, cover with boiling water, stand 20 minutes. Drain mushrooms, discard stems, slice caps.

Heat oil in large pan, add ginger, lemon grass, spices, sambal oelek and mushrooms, cook, stirring, until fragrant. Add coconut cream, crumbled stock cubes and water, bring to boil, add fish, cook, covered, about 10 minutes or until fish is just tender. Stir in bok choy, shallots and noodles; reheat gently.
Serves 4 to 6.

- ■ Recipe best made just before serving.
- ■ Freeze: Not suitable.
- ♣ Microwave: Noodles suitable.
- ♣ Slow cooker: Not suitable.
- ♣ Pressure cooker: Not suitable.
- ♣ Conventional oven: Not suitable.

ABOVE: Quick Lemon Grass and Coconut Fish Stew.
RIGHT: Cajun-Style Seafood Gumbo.

CAJUN-STYLE SEAFOOD GUMBO

250g okra
1 tablespoon olive oil
4 bacon rashers, chopped
800g boneless white fish fillets
1kg uncooked medium prawns
30g butter
1 medium (150g) onion,
    finely chopped
2 cloves garlic, crushed
1 tablespoon plain flour
425g can tomatoes
1 tablespoon tomato paste
1 teaspoon Tabasco sauce
2 teaspoons Worcestershire sauce
310g can corn kernels,
    rinsed, drained

FISH STOCK
1 litre (4 cups) water
1kg white fish heads
1 large (200g) onion, chopped
1 small (70g) carrot, chopped
½ cup (125ml) dry white wine
1 large fresh parsley sprig

Trim stems from okra; halve okra lengthways. Heat oil in pan, add bacon, cook, stirring, until bacon is crisp; drain on absorbent paper. Cut fish into 3cm pieces. Shell and devein prawns, leaving tails intact.

Heat butter in large pan, add onion and garlic, cook, stirring, until onion is soft. Add flour, cook, stirring, until lightly browned. Add reserved fish stock, undrained crushed tomatoes, paste, sauces, corn and okra, stir over heat until mixture boils, simmer, uncovered, 25 minutes, stirring occasionally. Add seafood and bacon, simmer, uncovered, about 5 minutes or until seafood is tender.

Fish Stock: Combine all ingredients in medium pan, simmer, uncovered, 20 minutes. Strain; reserve 1½ cups (375ml) stock for this recipe.

Serves 4 to 6.

■ Stock can be made a day ahead. Gumbo best made close to serving.
■ Storage: Covered, in refrigerator.
■ Freeze: Stock suitable.
♣ Microwave: Not suitable.
♣ Slow cooker: Not suitable.
♣ Pressure cooker: Not suitable.
♣ Conventional oven: Not suitable.

SQUID IN TOMATO WINE SAUCE

You will need to cook about 1 cup (200g) white long-grain rice for this recipe.

12 small (1.8kg) squid
2 x 425g cans tomatoes
1 cup (250ml) water
¾ cup (180ml) dry red wine
2 tablespoons tomato paste
2 tablespoons drained capers
1 clove garlic, crushed
2 tablespoons chopped fresh parsley

FILLING
2 teaspoons olive oil
1 small (80g) onion, finely chopped
2 medium (240g) zucchini, grated
1 clove garlic, crushed
3 cups cooked white long-grain rice
⅓ cup (50g) pine nuts, toasted
1 egg, lightly beaten
1 tablespoon chopped fresh basil
2 teaspoons balsamic vinegar

Gently pull head and entrails from squid; discard. Remove and discard clear backbone (quill) from inside body. Remove side flaps and firmly pull skin from squid hood with salted fingers. Wash hoods thoroughly. Fill hoods with filling, secure ends with toothpicks.

Combine undrained crushed tomatoes, water, wine, paste, capers and garlic in flameproof casserole dish (3 litre/12 cup capacity), bring to boil; simmer, uncovered, 10 minutes. Stir in parsley, then add squid in single layer. Bake, covered, in moderate oven about 1 hour or until squid are tender.

Filling: Heat oil in large pan, add onion, zucchini and garlic, cook, stirring, about 5 minutes or until onion is soft. Stir in remaining ingredients.
Serves 6.

- ■ Filling can be made a day ahead. Squid best filled and cooked close to serving.
- ■ Storage: Covered, in refrigerator.
- ■ Freeze: Not suitable.
- ● Microwave: Suitable.
- ● Slow cooker: Not suitable.
- ● Pressure cooker: Not suitable.
- ● Cook-top: Suitable.

QUICK 'N' EASY PRAWN CURRY

2kg uncooked large prawns
1 tablespoon peanut oil
10 green shallots, chopped
1 clove garlic, crushed
3 sticks celery, sliced
1½ tablespoons green curry paste
½ cup (125ml) fish stock
½ cup (125ml) water
400ml can coconut milk

Shell and devein prawns, leaving tails intact. Heat oil in pan, add shallots and garlic, cook, stirring, until shallots are soft. Add celery and paste, cook, stirring, 2 minutes. Stir in combined stock, water and half the coconut milk, simmer, uncovered, 15 minutes. Add prawns to pan, simmer, stirring, about 5 minutes or until prawns are tender. Add remaining coconut milk, stir until heated through; do not boil.
Serves 4.

- ■ Recipe best made close to serving.
- ■ Freeze: Not suitable.
- ● Microwave: Suitable.
- ● Slow cooker: Not suitable.
- ● Pressure cooker: Not suitable.
- ● Conventional oven: Not suitable.

LEFT: Squid in Tomato Wine Sauce.
BELOW: Quick 'n' Easy Prawn Curry.

Below: Plate from Sahba; tiles from Country Floors.

Vegetarian

You can't go wrong putting vegetables together in these quick and easy recipes. Tonight, for example, you can lift the lid on a steaming, fragrant vegetable curry, spicy vegetable gumbo or stylish and irresistible pepper casserole. Other recipes have tasty toppings, such as pasta and cheese, lentils and polenta or hot potato scones. Together with grains and pulses for energy and protein, the recipes make healthful, complete meals, or superb accompaniments, if you prefer.

SPICY OKRA, CORN AND PEPPER GUMBO

800g okra
1½ tablespoons olive oil
2 medium (300g) onions, chopped
4 cloves garlic, crushed
1½ teaspoons Cajun seasoning
1 teaspoon ground cumin
¼ teaspoon cayenne pepper
3 sticks celery, chopped
2 large (700g) green peppers, chopped
2 large (700g) red peppers, chopped
2 fresh corn cobs, chopped
½ bunch (10) baby carrots, chopped
2 cups (500ml) vegetable stock
2 x 425g cans tomatoes
2 tablespoons Worcestershire sauce
½ cup (100g) basmati rice
¼ cup chopped fresh parsley

Trim stems from okra; discard stems. Heat oil in large heavy-based pan, add onions, garlic and spices, cook, stirring, until onions are soft. Add vegetables, stock, undrained crushed tomatoes and sauce, simmer, covered, 30 minutes. Add rice and okra, simmer, covered, about 25 minutes or until rice is tender. Serve sprinkled with parsley.
Serves 6.

■ Recipe can be made a day ahead.
■ Storage: Covered, in refrigerator.
■ Freeze: Not suitable.
♣ Microwave: Suitable.
♣ Slow cooker: Not suitable.
♣ Pressure cooker: Suitable.
♣ Conventional oven: Suitable.

RIGHT: Spicy Okra, Corn and Pepper Gumbo.

RED LENTIL AND VEGETABLE STEW

4 medium (480g) zucchini
4 (240g) finger eggplants
1 medium (200g) red pepper
2 tablespoons olive oil
2 cloves garlic, crushed
1 medium (350g) leek, sliced
1 teaspoon caraway seeds
1 teaspoon cumin seeds
2 x 425g cans tomatoes
1/3 cup (80ml) dry red wine
1 teaspoon sugar
1/4 cup (60ml) tomato paste
1 cup (200g) red lentils
2 cups (500ml) vegetable stock
1 tablespoon chopped fresh basil

Halve zucchini and eggplants lengthways. Quarter pepper, remove seeds and membranes. Heat 1 tablespoon of the oil in griddle pan, add vegetables in batches, cook until browned on both sides; remove from pan.

Heat remaining oil in large pan, add garlic, leek and seeds, cook, stirring, until leek is soft. Add undrained crushed tomatoes, wine, sugar, paste and lentils, simmer, uncovered, 5 minutes. Stir in stock, basil and vegetables, simmer, uncovered, about 15 minutes or until vegetables are tender.
Serves 4.

■ Recipe can be made a day ahead.
■ Storage: Covered, in refrigerator.
■ Freeze: Not suitable.
♣ Microwave: Tomato lentil mixture suitable; add vegetables just before serving.
♣ Slow cooker: Not suitable.
♣ Pressure cooker: Not suitable.
♣ Conventional oven: Tomato lentil mixture suitable; add vegetables just before serving.

LEFT: Red Lentil and Vegetable Stew.
ABOVE: Kumara and Potatoes in Peanut Coconut Sauce.

KUMARA AND POTATOES IN PEANUT COCONUT SAUCE

2 medium (800g) kumara
1 tablespoon peanut oil
2 medium (300g) onions, sliced
2 cloves garlic, crushed
1 teaspoon grated fresh ginger
1/2 teaspoon sambal oelek
1 tablespoon mild curry powder
1 teaspoon ground cumin
1 teaspoon ground coriander
1 tablespoon soy sauce
1/2 cup (130g) smooth peanut butter
2 1/2 cups (625ml) vegetable stock

1 cup (250ml) coconut milk
12 baby (480g) new potatoes, halved
3/4 cup (150g) red lentils
1 tablespoon chopped fresh
  coriander

Cut kumara into 3cm pieces. Heat oil in large pan, add onions, garlic, ginger, sambal oelek and spices, cook, stirring, until fragrant. Add sauce, peanut butter, stock, coconut milk and potatoes, simmer, covered, 5 minutes. Add lentils and kumara, simmer, covered, stirring often, about 20 minutes or until vegetables are tender. Serve sprinkled with fresh coriander.

Serves 4.

■ Recipe can be made a day ahead.
■ Storage: Covered, in refrigerator.
■ Freeze: Not suitable.
🥄 Microwave: Suitable.
🥄 Slow cooker: Not suitable.
🥄 Pressure cooker: Not suitable.
🥄 Conventional oven: Suitable.

VINDALOO VEGETABLES

1 tablespoon vegetable oil
2 medium (300g) onions,
  roughly chopped
2 cloves garlic, crushed
1/4 cup (60ml) vindaloo curry paste
12 baby (480g) new potatoes
800g pumpkin, roughly chopped
1 large (350g) red pepper,
  roughly chopped
3 medium (360g) carrots,
  roughly chopped
1/4 medium (400g) cauliflower,
  chopped
1 1/2 cups (375ml) vegetable stock
425ml can coconut milk
2 dried lime leaves
1/3 cup (50g) dried currants
3 fresh corn cobs, chopped
3 medium (350g) zucchini,
  roughly chopped
400g broccoli, chopped
1/4 cup (35g) chopped roasted
  unsalted peanuts

Heat oil in large pan, add onions and garlic, cook, stirring, until onions are soft. Add curry paste, cook, stirring, until fragrant. Add potatoes, pumpkin, pepper, carrots, cauliflower, stock, coconut milk, lime leaves and currants, simmer, covered, 20 minutes. Stir in corn, zucchini and broccoli, simmer, covered, about 20 minutes or until vegetables are tender. Serve sprinkled with peanuts.

Serves 4 to 6.

■ Recipe can be made a day ahead.
■ Storage: Covered, in refrigerator.
■ Freeze: Suitable.

♣ Microwave: Suitable.
♣ Slow cooker: Not suitable.
♣ Pressure cooker: Not suitable.
♣ Conventional oven: Suitable.

HERBED VEGETABLES WITH PASTA CHEESE TOPPING

1/3 cup (80ml) olive oil
3 cloves garlic, crushed
1/4 cup chopped fresh basil
1 tablespoon chopped fresh
  rosemary
2 medium (600g) eggplants
coarse cooking salt
1 large (500g) kumara,
  peeled, sliced
4 medium (480g) zucchini,
  thinly sliced
2 medium (300g) onions,
  thinly sliced
2 medium (260g) tomatoes,
  thinly sliced

PASTA CHEESE TOPPING
250g small pasta shells
1 1/2 cups (185g) grated tasty
  cheddar cheese
1/4 cup (50g) sunflower seed
  kernels, toasted

Combine oil, garlic and herbs in small bowl. Cut eggplants into 7mm slices, place on wire racks over oven trays, sprinkle with salt, stand 30 minutes. Rinse under cold water; pat dry with absorbent paper.

Place half the eggplant slices over base of shallow ovenproof dish (4 litre/16 cup capacity). Brush with a little oil mixture, top with kumara, zucchini, onions, tomatoes and remaining eggplants, brush with remaining oil mixture. Press vegetable mixture down firmly, spoon over pasta cheese topping. Bake, covered, in moderately hot oven 1 hour, remove cover, bake about 30 minutes or until browned.

Pasta Cheese Topping: Add pasta to large pan of boiling water, boil, uncovered, until just tender; drain, rinse under cold water, drain. Combine pasta, cheese and kernels in bowl; mix well.
Serves 6.

■ Recipe best made close to serving.
■ Freeze: Not suitable.

♣ Microwave: Pasta suitable.
♣ Slow cooker: Not suitable.
♣ Pressure cooker: Not suitable.
♣ Cook-top: Not suitable.

ABOVE: Herbed Vegetables with Pasta Cheese Topping.
RIGHT: Vindaloo Vegetables.

BAKED EGGPLANTS, TOMATO AND CHICKPEAS

2 medium (600g) eggplants, sliced
2 tablespoons olive oil
10 (250g) spring onions, trimmed
2 cloves garlic, crushed
3 sticks celery, sliced
2 x 310g cans chickpeas,
   rinsed, drained
4 large (1kg) tomatoes,
   peeled, chopped
½ cup (125ml) vegetable stock
¼ cup chopped fresh parsley
¼ cup chopped fresh oregano
1 tablespoon tomato paste
1 bunch (340g) baby bok choy,
   chopped

Place eggplant slices on greased oven tray, brush lightly with about half the oil, grill until browned on both sides. Heat remaining oil in flameproof casserole dish (3 litre/12 cup capacity), add onions, cook, stirring, until onions are lightly browned. Stir in eggplants, garlic, celery, chickpeas, tomatoes, stock and herbs. Bake, covered, in moderate oven about 45 minutes or until vegetables are tender. Remove from oven, stir in paste and bok choy just before serving.

Serves 4.

■ Recipe can be made a day ahead.
■ Storage: Covered, in refrigerator.
■ Freeze: Not suitable.
♣ Microwave: Suitable.
♣ Slow cooker: Not suitable.
♣ Pressure cooker: Not suitable.
♣ Cook-top: Suitable.

RATATOUILLE CASSEROLE

2 tablespoons olive oil
2 cloves garlic, crushed
1 small (200g) leek, chopped
1 small (230g) eggplant, chopped
2 medium (400g) green peppers,
   chopped
2 medium (400g) red peppers,
   chopped
2 medium (240g) zucchini, chopped
200g button mushrooms, halved
1/4 cup (60ml) dry white wine
2 x 425g cans tomatoes
1/2 cup (125ml) tomato puree
200g green beans, chopped
2 teaspoons sugar
1 tablespoon chopped fresh oregano
2 tablespoons grated parmesan
   cheese

LENTIL POLENTA TOPPING
1/2 cup (100g) red lentils
1 cup (250ml) milk
1 1/2 cups (375ml) vegetable stock
1 1/2 cups (375ml) water
1 cup (170g) polenta
1/2 cup (40g) grated parmesan cheese
1 tablespoon chopped fresh parsley

Heat oil in large flameproof casserole dish (3 litre/12 cup capacity), add garlic and leek, cook, stirring, until leek is soft. Add eggplant, peppers, zucchini, mushrooms and wine, cook, stirring, until liquid is reduced by half. Add undrained crushed tomatoes, puree, beans, sugar and oregano, simmer, uncovered, about 20 minutes or until sauce is slightly thickened. Add lentil polenta topping, sprinkle with cheese, bake, uncovered, in moderate oven about 20 minutes or until browned.

Lentil Polenta Topping: Lightly grease 26cm x 32cm Swiss roll pan, line base and sides with baking paper. Add lentils to pan of boiling water, boil, uncovered, about 10 minutes or until tender; drain.

Combine milk, stock and water in large pan, bring to boil, add polenta, stir over heat about 10 minutes or until mixture is thick; stir in cheese, lentils and parsley. Press mixture into prepared pan, cool, cover, refrigerate until cold. Turn onto board, cut into 5cm shapes. Serves 6 to 8.

■ Lentil polenta topping can be made a day ahead.
■ Storage: Covered, in refrigerator.
■ Freeze: Not suitable.

▲ Microwave: Not suitable.
▲ Slow cooker: Not suitable.
▲ Pressure cooker: Not suitable.
▲ Cook-top: Not suitable.

ABOVE: Ratatouille Casserole.
RIGHT: Baked Eggplants, Tomato and Chickpeas.

Above: Setting from House. Right: Bowl and serviettes from The Bay Tree Kitchen Shop.

TRIPLE BEAN CASSEROLE WITH POTATO SCONES

You will need to cook about 3 medium (600g) potatoes for this recipe.

½ cup (100g) dried pinto beans
½ cup (100g) dried red kidney beans
2 teaspoons vegetable oil
1 large (200g) onion, sliced
1 litre (4 cups) vegetable stock
2 teaspoons Cajun seasoning
1 teaspoon ground cumin
1 medium (200g) red pepper,
　　chopped
1 medium (200g) yellow pepper,
　　chopped
2 (120g) finger eggplants, sliced
2 small (180g) zucchini, sliced
250g asparagus, chopped
150g green beans, chopped
1 cup (140g) frozen corn kernels
6 medium (780g) tomatoes,
　　peeled, chopped

POTATO SCONES
1¼ cups (185g) self-raising flour
¼ cup (40g) polenta
60g butter, chopped
1 tablespoon chopped fresh basil
¼ cup (30g) grated tasty
　　cheddar cheese
1¼ cups mashed potato
¼ cup (60ml) milk, approximately

Place pinto and kidney beans in bowl, cover well with water; cover, stand overnight.

　Drain beans. Heat oil in flameproof casserole dish (3 litre/12 cup capacity), add onion, cook, stirring, until onion is soft. Add pinto and kidney beans and stock, simmer, covered, 1 hour. Add spices and vegetables, simmer, covered, 5 minutes. Top with scones, brush lightly with a little milk, bake, uncovered, in moderate oven about 35 minutes or until scones are browned.

Potato Scones: Combine flour and polenta in bowl, rub in butter. Stir in basil, cheese, potato and enough milk to mix to a soft dough. Turn dough onto lightly floured surface, knead until smooth. Roll dough to 1.5cm thickness, cut into 4cm rounds.
Serves 4 to 6.

■ Casserole can be made a day
　 ahead. Scones best made just
　 before serving.
■ Storage: Covered, in refrigerator.
■ Freeze: Not suitable.

🌳 Microwave: Not suitable.
🌳 Slow cooker: Not suitable.
🌳 Pressure cooker: Not suitable.
🌳 Conventional oven: Not suitable.

RIGHT: Triple Bean Casserole with Potato Scones.

Fabric and bowl from Morris Home & Garden Wares.

PEPPER CASSEROLE WITH ZUCCHINI AND BEANS

½ cup (100g) dried borlotti beans
4 medium (800g) red peppers
4 medium (480g) zucchini, chopped
4 baby (100g) onions, quartered
200g green beans, halved
310g can chickpeas, rinsed, drained
2 tablespoons olive oil
¼ cup (20g) parmesan cheese flakes

TOMATO SAUCE
2 x 425g cans tomatoes
1 tablespoon balsamic vinegar
½ teaspoon sugar
¼ cup shredded fresh basil

Place borlotti beans in large bowl, cover well with water; cover, stand overnight.

Drain borlotti beans, add to pan of boiling water, simmer, uncovered, about 20 minutes or until tender; drain. Halve peppers lengthways, remove seeds and membranes. Place peppers, cut side up, in shallow ovenproof dish (3 litre/ 12 cup capacity). Combine borlotti beans, zucchini, onions, green beans, chickpeas and oil in bowl, mix well; spoon into peppers, pour over tomato sauce. Bake, covered, in moderate oven 1 hour, remove cover, bake about 15 minutes or until peppers are tender. Serve topped with cheese flakes.

Tomato Sauce: Combine undrained crushed tomatoes, vinegar and sugar in pan, simmer, uncovered, about 5 minutes or until sauce is slightly thickened. Stir in basil.
Serves 4.

■ Peppers and sauce can be made a day ahead.
■ Storage: Covered, separately, in refrigerator.
■ Freeze: Not suitable.
♣ Microwave: Suitable.
♣ Slow cooker: Not suitable.
♣ Pressure cooker: Not suitable.
♣ Cook-top: Not suitable.

BUTTER BEANS AND PASTA WITH PESTO

1.75 litres (7 cups) vegetable stock
500g tri-coloured spiral pasta
1 medium (200g) red pepper, sliced
2 cups firmly packed fresh
**   basil leaves**
1 cup (100g) walnuts
5 cloves garlic, crushed
2 x 310g cans butter beans,
**   rinsed, drained**
1/4 cup (60ml) cream
2/3 cup (80g) grated tasty
**   cheddar cheese**
2/3 cup (50g) grated parmesan cheese

Bring stock to boil in large pan, add pasta and pepper, boil, uncovered, until pasta is just tender; do not drain. Blend or process basil, nuts and garlic until smooth, stir into pasta mixture with beans and cream. Spoon mixture into shallow ovenproof dish (3.5 litre/ 14 cup capacity).

Sprinkle with combined cheeses, bake, uncovered, in moderate oven about 15 minutes or until browned. Serves 4 to 6.

■ Recipe best made just before serving.
■ Freeze: Not suitable.

● Microwave: Pasta mixture suitable.
● Slow cooker: Not suitable.
● Pressure cooker: Not suitable.
● Cook-top: Not suitable.

LEFT: Pepper Casserole with Zucchini and Beans.
BELOW: Butter Beans and Pasta with Pesto.

Left: Cutlery from Villeroy & Boch.

Something Different

If you are planning a dinner party, make one of these main dishes your pièce de résistance; they are all fabulous! Rabbit is super smart to serve these days and is a very flavoursome meat. In this section, we have also made confit of duck — a French classic — easy, as well as authentic. Equally interesting recipes include kangaroo, quail and turkey, all perfect for entertaining.

RABBIT WITH PORT, ORANGE AND SAGE

1.5kg rabbit pieces
plain flour
2 tablespoons vegetable oil
2 large (400g) onions, quartered
4 cloves garlic, crushed
½ cup (125ml) orange juice
½ cup (125ml) port
1 cup (250ml) dry red wine
2 tablespoons redcurrant jelly
1 medium (180g) orange, sliced
10 small fresh sage leaves
1 cup (250ml) chicken stock

Toss rabbit pieces in flour, shake away excess flour. Heat half the oil in flame-proof casserole dish (1.75 litre/7 cup capacity), add rabbit in batches, cook until browned on both sides; remove from dish.

Heat remaining oil in same dish, add onions and garlic, cook, stirring, until onions are soft. Add rabbit and remaining ingredients, bake, covered, in moderately slow oven about 1½ hours or until rabbit is tender.
Serves 4 to 6.

■ Recipe can be made a day ahead.
■ Storage: Covered, in refrigerator.
■ Freeze: Suitable.

🍲 Microwave: Not suitable.
🍲 Slow cooker: Suitable.
🍲 Pressure cooker: Suitable.
🍲 Cook-top: Suitable.

RIGHT: Rabbit with Port, Orange and Sage.

112

ANISE AND GINGER BRAISED DUCK

1.7kg duck
1/4 cup (60ml) sweet sherry
1 cup (250ml) water
2 tablespoons soy sauce
4 cloves garlic, sliced
3cm piece fresh ginger, sliced
3 star anise
1 teaspoon sambal oelek
1 teaspoon cornflour
2 teaspoons water, extra
1 green shallot, chopped

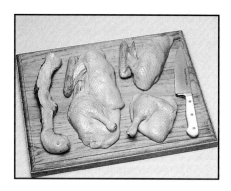

Using knife or poultry shears, cut down either side of backbone; discard. Cut duck in half through breastbone, then cut each half into 2 pieces. Trim excess fat from duck, leaving skin intact.

Place duck pieces in single layer, skin side down, in large pan, cook over low heat about 10 minutes or until skin is crisp; drain on absorbent paper. Place duck in clean pan, add sherry, water, sauce, garlic, ginger, star anise and sambal oelek, simmer, covered, about 1 1/2 hours or until duck is very tender. Turn duck halfway through cooking. Cover undrained duck mixture, refrigerate overnight.

Next day, discard fat layer from surface. Place duck mixture in pan, cover, cook over low heat until duck is heated through. Remove duck from pan; keep warm. Strain liquid into small pan, stir in blended cornflour and extra water, stir over heat until mixture boils and thickens slightly. Serve sauce over duck, sprinkle with shallot.
Serves 4.

■ Recipe must be made a day ahead.
■ Storage: Covered, in refrigerator.
■ Freeze: Suitable.
♣ Microwave: Not suitable.
♣ Slow cooker: Suitable.
♣ Pressure cooker: Suitable.
♣ Conventional oven: Suitable.

DUCK WITH LEEKS, SAGE AND ROSEMARY

2kg duck pieces
plain flour
2 small (400g) leeks
2 sticks celery
2 tablespoons olive oil
6 slices (90g) pancetta, sliced
2 cloves garlic, crushed
1 1/4 cups (310ml) chicken stock
1/2 cup (125ml) dry white wine
2 teaspoons chopped fresh sage
4 sprigs fresh rosemary

Remove and discard skin from duck pieces. Toss duck in flour; shake away excess flour. Cut leeks and celery into 6cm lengths, then into thick strips. Heat half the oil in pan, add duck in batches, cook until browned on both sides; remove from pan. Heat remaining oil in same pan, add leeks, celery, pancetta and garlic, cook, stirring, until leeks are soft. Add stock, wine, herbs and duck, simmer, covered, about 1 hour or until duck is tender, stirring occasionally.
Serves 4.

■ Recipe can be made a day ahead.
■ Storage: Covered, in refrigerator.
■ Freeze: Suitable.
♣ Microwave: Not suitable.
♣ Slow cooker: Suitable.
♣ Pressure cooker: Suitable.
♣ Conventional oven: Suitable.

LEFT: Anise and Ginger Braised Duck.
RIGHT: Duck with Leeks, Sage and Rosemary.

Right: Tiles from Country Floors.

MARINATED KANGAROO WITH BACON AND POTATOES

1.5kg kangaroo rump
2 tablespoons olive oil
4 bacon rashers, roughly chopped
2 medium (300g) onions,
  roughly chopped
6 medium (780g) tomatoes, peeled,
  roughly chopped
1 cup (250ml) beef stock
12 baby (480g) new potatoes
1 tablespoon chopped fresh sage

MARINADE
½ cup (125ml) dry red wine
2 cloves garlic, crushed
2 bay leaves

Cut kangaroo into 4cm pieces, combine with marinade in bowl, cover; refrigerate several hours or overnight.

Drain kangaroo, reserve marinade. Heat half the oil in pan, add kangaroo in batches, cook until browned; remove from pan. Heat remaining oil in same pan, add bacon and onions, cook, stirring, until onions are soft. Add tomatoes, cook, stirring, about 5 minutes or until tomatoes are soft. Return kangaroo to pan with reserved marinade, stock, potatoes and sage, simmer, covered, 1½ hours, remove cover, simmer 30 minutes or until kangaroo is tender, stirring occasionally. Discard bay leaves.

Marinade: Combine all ingredients in bowl; mix well.

Serves 4 to 6.

■ Recipe can be made a day ahead.
■ Storage: Covered, in refrigerator.
■ Freeze: Suitable.

♣ Microwave: Not suitable.
♣ Slow cooker: Suitable.
♣ Pressure cooker: Suitable.
♣ Conventional oven: Suitable.

RIGHT: Confit of Duck with Peach Chutney.
BELOW: Marinated Kangaroo with Bacon and Potatoes.

Right: China from Waterford Wedgwood; cutlery from Villeroy & Boch.

CONFIT OF DUCK WITH PEACH CHUTNEY

A confit is a method of preserving where goose, duck, turkey or pork is cooked slowly in its own fat. Here, we have supplemented duck fat with lard. Choose a large, shallow ovenproof dish so that duck pieces can be packed in a single layer and covered with the fat mixture at all stages. The fat mixture may be re-used for a similar recipe, if it is clarified before re-using.

2 x 1.7kg ducks
1 tablespoon sea salt
2 tablespoons chopped fresh thyme
4 cloves garlic, flattened
12 black peppercorns
500g lard, chopped

PEACH CHUTNEY
4 medium (800g) peaches
1 medium (150g) onion,
  finely chopped
1 tablespoon chopped fresh thyme
1 cup (200g) firmly packed
  brown sugar
3/4 cup (180ml) white wine vinegar
1 large (150g) apple, chopped
2 tablespoons chopped dried figs
1/4 teaspoon ground ginger

Place 1 duck on board, breast side up. Cut thigh and leg portions from duck.

Cut along 1 side of breastbone, cutting down alongside the wish bone. Slide knife between breast and bone, remove breast (with skin) from bone; repeat with other side. Repeat procedure with remaining duck. Discard carcasses.

Remove skin and fat from legs; discard skin, reserve fat. Place duck pieces in shallow ovenproof dish, sprinkle with salt, thyme, garlic and peppercorns, cover, refrigerate 30 minutes.

Combine lard and reserved duck fat in large pan, heat until melted, add duck pieces, bring to boil; remove from heat.

Return duck pieces to shallow oven-proof dish in a single layer, carefully pour over hot fat mixture, making sure the duck pieces are completely covered.

Bake, covered, in moderately slow oven about 2 hours or until duck is very tender; cool to room temperature; discard garlic. Refrigerate duck, covered, for at least 3 days before serving.

To serve, remove duck pieces as required; remove as much excess fat as possible. Place duck on oven tray, grill until heated through and skin is crisp. Serve with peach chutney.

Peach Chutney: Add peaches to large pan of boiling water, boil, uncovered, 1 minute; drain, rinse under cold water; drain. Peel away skins. Halve peaches, discard stones, chop peaches roughly. Combine peaches with remaining ingredients in medium pan, stir over heat, without boiling, until sugar is dissolved. Bring to boil, simmer, uncovered, stirring occasionally, about 30 minutes or until mixture is thick. Pour mixture into hot sterilised jar (2 cup/500ml capacity); seal while hot.
Serves 4 to 6.

■ Duck can be made 1 month ahead. Peach chutney can be made 3 months ahead.
■ Storage: Duck, covered, in refrigerator; chutney, in cool, dark place.
■ Freeze: Not suitable.
♣ Microwave: Chutney suitable.
♣ Slow cooker: Not suitable.
♣ Pressure cooker: Not suitable.
♣ Cook-top: Duck not suitable.

BRAISED TURKEY WITH MUSHROOMS AND APRICOTS

3kg turkey
plain flour
¼ cup (60ml) olive oil
2 medium (300g) onions, sliced
1 clove garlic, crushed
250g button mushrooms
1 cup (150g) dried apricots
1 medium (200g) red pepper, sliced
¼ cup (60ml) dry white wine
2 cups (500ml) chicken stock
425ml can apricot nectar
1 tablespoon chopped fresh parsley

Using a knife or poultry shears, cut down either side of backbone; discard backbone. Cut turkey in half through breastbone, then cut each half into even-sized portions.

Toss turkey pieces in flour, shake away excess flour. Heat half the oil in large pan, add turkey in batches, cook until browned all over; drain on absorbent paper. Heat remaining oil in same pan, add onions, garlic, mush-rooms, apricots and pepper, cook, stirring, until onions are soft. Add wine, cook, stirring, until most of the liquid has evaporated. Return turkey to pan, add stock and nectar, stir until combined. Simmer, covered, about 40 minutes or until turkey is tender. Serve sprinkled with parsley.
Serves 8.

■ Recipe can be made a day ahead.
■ Storage: Covered, in refrigerator.
■ Freeze: Suitable.

♣ Microwave: Not suitable.
♣ Slow cooker: Suitable.
♣ Pressure cooker: Suitable.
♣ Conventional oven: Suitable.

RIGHT: Roast Quail with Sage and Bacon.
BELOW: Braised Turkey with Mushrooms and Apricots.

ROAST QUAIL WITH SAGE AND BACON

12 quail
12 fresh sage leaves
12 bacon rashers
2 tablespoons olive oil
2 cloves garlic, crushed
1 small (200g) leek, chopped
300g button mushrooms, sliced
1 tablespoon plain flour
1/4 cup (60ml) dry white wine
3/4 cup (180ml) chicken stock
425g can tomato puree
1 teaspoon sugar
1 tablespoon chopped fresh parsley

Tuck wings under quail, bend legs back to insert into wings. Wrap each quail in sage and bacon, secure with toothpicks. Heat oil in baking dish, add quail in batches, cook until lightly browned all over; drain on absorbent paper.

Add garlic, leek and mushrooms to dish, cook, stirring, until leek is soft. Add flour, cook, stirring, 1 minute. Add wine and stock, cook, stirring, until liquid is reduced by half. Stir in puree and sugar. Return quail to dish, bake, covered, in hot oven 30 minutes. Remove cover, bake about 10 minutes or until quail are tender. Serve sprinkled with parsley. Serves 6.

■ Recipe can be made a day ahead.
■ Storage: Covered, in refrigerator.
■ Freeze: Not suitable.

♣ Microwave: Not suitable.
♣ Slow cooker: Not suitable.
♣ Pressure cooker: Not suitable.
♣ Cook-top: Not suitable.

119

CREAMY RABBIT WITH FRESH TARRAGON

1.7kg rabbit cutlets
plain flour
2 tablespoons olive oil
5 cloves garlic, crushed
2 tablespoons brown sugar
10 (250g) spring onions,
    trimmed, halved
1 tablespoon white wine vinegar
1 cup (250ml) dry white wine
1 cup (250ml) chicken stock
2 tablespoons chopped fresh
    tarragon
½ cup (125ml) cream
1 tablespoon chopped fresh
    tarragon, extra

Toss rabbit in flour, shake away excess flour. Heat oil in flameproof casserole dish (3 litre/12 cup capacity), add rabbit in batches, cook until browned on both sides; drain on absorbent paper.

Add garlic to same dish, cook, stirring, until lightly browned. Add sugar, onions and vinegar, cook 5 minutes. Stir in wine, stock and tarragon, bring to boil; add rabbit, bake, covered, in moderate oven about 2 hours or until rabbit is tender. Remove rabbit and onions from dish, keep warm.

Transfer cooking liquid to clean pan, bring to boil, simmer, uncovered, 5 minutes. Stir in cream and extra tarragon, stir until hot. Serve sauce over rabbit.

Serves 6.

■ Recipe best made just before serving.
■ Freeze: Suitable; stir in cream and tarragon when reheating.
♣ Microwave: Not suitable.
♣ Slow cooker: Suitable.
♣ Pressure cooker: Suitable.
♣ Cook-top: Suitable.

BELOW: Creamy Rabbit with Fresh Tarragon.

Casserole Basics

Most of our recipes can be adapted to cook either in the oven or on the cook-top, many are suitable for a slow cooker or pressure cooker, and some are suitable for a microwave oven. Whichever way you cook, we suggest these guidelines to help you:

Cookware

● Casserole cookware is available in a large variety of shapes, sizes and finishes. Some casserole dishes are only ovenproof, while others are flameproof.
● Ovenproof dishes can be used in the oven without breaking; these include earthenware, china, glass and some types of clay pottery.
● Flameproof dishes can be used in the oven as well as on the cook-top; these include cast iron and stainless steel dishes. Cast iron dishes retain higher heat than most other cookware, so cooking time and temperature may need to be reduced slightly.
● Ensure casserole cookware lids are tight-fitting when food is cooked covered, or cover tightly with foil.
● Our recipes give you the approximate litre/cup capacity for cookware. The shape doesn't matter. However, if cookware is too small the food may boil over; if cookware is too large the food may dry out.

Oven Cooking

● As a rule, cooking time in the oven will be longer than on the cook-top. Simply continue to cook until the meat is tender, or follow guidelines in the recipe. Choose ovenproof cookware, unless any part of the recipe requires a flameproof dish.

Cook-top Cooking

● As a rule, food needs less time on the cook-top than in the oven; you need to check at intervals. Choose flameproof cookware that is heavy-based and will sit flat on an electric cook-top.
● Make use of a simmer mat (pictured at right) on a gas burner, so the flame can be dispersed evenly and kept low.

Slow Cooker

● As a guide, recipes are suitable for a slow cooker where long, slow oven or cook-top cooking is specified.
● Before you begin, it is important to read the manufacturer's instructions thoroughly. Always follow all safety precautions.
● Always cover a slow cooker with its lid; do not lift the lid too often during cooking.
● Slow cookers do not allow food to reach a high temperature; the food is meant to be cooked over a long period of time – up to about 8 hours.
● It is not essential to brown meat or vegetables beforehand, just combine all ingredients in the cooker.
● Add cream, milk, sour cream or yogurt at the end of cooking time.

Pressure Cooker

● Many of our recipes can be adapted to cook in a pressure cooker; check the note at the end of each recipe. We have said "not suitable" when casseroles cook in about 30 to 40 minutes, particularly those containing seafood and chicken.
● Before you begin, it is important to read the manufacturer's instructions thoroughly. Always follow all safety precautions.
● You may need to refer to the recipe booklet supplied by the manufacturer to work out the cooking time for the recipes you select from this book.

● Recipes with a high liquid content usually work best for pressure cookers.
● Never fill the pressure cooker more than two-thirds full.
● As a rule, cooking time can be reduced to about a third. For example, if a casserole is cooked in the oven for 1 hour, it could be expected to cook in a pressure cooker in about 20 minutes.
● Thicken with cornflour, etc., and add herbs and green vegetables after the meat or chicken is tender, or just before serving. Simply remove the lid and use the pressure cooker like a saucepan.

Microwave Cooking

● Most casseroles can be cooked in the microwave oven, but we prefer the longer, slower cooking methods.
● Follow the manufacturer's instructions when using your microwave, and always follow all safety precautions.
● A combination of convection and microwave cooking will give good results.

Freezing

● A lot of our casserole recipes may be too large in quantity for your family. In this case, why not cook half and freeze the other half for later? It is important to cool the food quickly before freezing.
● According to guidelines from CSIRO Australia, hot food should be covered, then placed directly in the refrigerator to cool. Modern refrigerators can cope with the load. First, place the hot dish on a heatproof tray, to protect the refrigerator shelf.
● Do not over-fill the container, but allow about 3cm for expansion. Food can then be frozen for up to 2 months. After reheating, add green vegetables, dairy products and any flour-based thickening.

Glossary

Here are some terms, names and alternatives to help everyone use and understand our recipes perfectly.

ALCOHOLIC CIDER: a fermented beverage made from apples.

ALLSPICE: pimento.

ARTICHOKE, GLOBE: large flower head of a plant from the thistle family.

BACON RASHERS: bacon slices.

BEEF: any cuts of beef suitable for stewing are also suitable for casseroles; these include blade steak and chuck steak, as listed here, plus gravy beef, rib steak and skirt steak.

Blade steak: a cut from the shoulder blade area.

Brisket: from the under section of the forequarter and ribs, rolled and secured with string or netting.

Chuck steak: from the neck area; can be used as 1 piece or as steak.

Fresh silverside: from the outside of the upper hind leg. Eye of silverside is a cylindrical portion of the silverside.

Minced: ground beef.

Spare ribs: we used the shorter spare ribs which are quite lean but meaty; these are also known as baby back ribs.

BEETROOT: regular round beet.

BELACAN (also belachan and blachan): dried shrimp paste sold in slabs or flat cakes.

BOK CHOY: known as Chinese chard.

Bok choy

Baby bok choy

BREADCRUMBS:

Packaged: use fine packaged crumbs.

Stale: use 1- or 2-day-old bread made into crumbs by grating, blending or processing.

BUTTER: use salted or unsalted (also called sweet) butter; 125g is equal to 1 stick butter.

CAJUN SEASONING: a combination of dried ingredients consisting of salt, peppers, garlic, onion and spices.

CAPERS: pickled buds of a Mediterranean shrub.

CELERIAC: tuberous root with brown skin, white flesh and a celery-like flavour.

CHEESE:

Bocconcini: small balls of mild, delicate cheese packaged in water or whey to keep them white and soft; any yellowing indicates they are old.

Feta: soft Greek cheese with a sharp, salty taste.

Parmesan: sharp-tasting hard cheese used as a flavour accent. We prefer to use fresh parmesan cheese, although it is available already finely grated.

Tasty cheddar: matured cheddar; use a hard, good-tasting variety.

CHESTNUTS: sweet, floury kernels.

CHICKEN:

Breast: with skin and bone intact.

Breast fillet: no skin and bones.

Drumstick: leg with skin intact.

Lovely leg: also known as drummette. Skinless drumstick with the end of the bone removed.

Maryland: leg and thigh with skin intact.

Thigh: has skin and bone intact.

Thigh cutlet: has skin and centre bone intact; sometimes called a chicken chop.

Thigh fillet: no skin and bones.

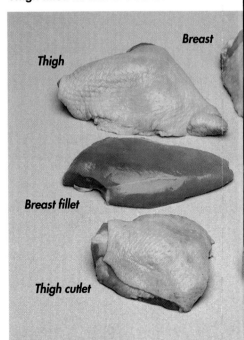

Breast

Thigh

Breast fillet

Thigh cutlet

CHILLIES: available in many different types and sizes. Use rubber gloves when chopping fresh chillies as they can burn your skin.

COCONUT: use desiccated coconut, unless otherwise specified.

Cream: available in cans and cartons from supermarkets.

Milk: available in cans and cartons from supermarkets.

CORNFLOUR: cornstarch.

CORNMEAL: ground corn (maize); similar to polenta but pale yellow and finer. One can be substituted for the other, but results will vary.

CORN RELISH: thick spread consisting of corn, celery, onion, capsicum, spices and mustard.

COUSCOUS: a fine cereal made from semolina.

CREAM: fresh pouring cream; has a minimum fat content of 35 per cent.

Sour: a thick commercially cultured soured cream.

Thickened (whipping): has a minimum fat content of 35 per cent, and includes a thickener.

CREME FRAICHE: available in cartons from delicatessens and supermarkets.

To make creme fraiche: combine 300ml cream with 300ml sour cream in bowl, cover, stand at room temperature until mixture is thick; this will take 1 or 2 days, depending on room temperature. Refrigerate before using. Makes about 2½ cups (625ml).

CUMQUATS: orange-coloured citrus fruit about the size of walnuts. Usually preserved or used for making jam, the fruit is always used unpeeled.

EGGPLANT: aubergine.

FENNEL: has a slight aniseed taste when fresh, ground or in seed form. The bulb can be eaten uncooked in salads or braised, steamed or stir-fried.

FISH SAUCE: made from the liquid drained from salted, fermented anchovies. Has a strong smell and taste; use sparingly. Several varieties are available and the intensity of flavour varies. We used Thai fish sauce.

FIVE SPICE POWDER: a pungent mixture of ground spices which includes cinnamon, cloves, fennel, star anise and Szechwan peppers.

FLOUR:

White plain: all-purpose flour.

GHEE: a pure butter fat available in plastic containers and cans, it can be heated to high temperatures without burning because of the lack of salts and milk solids.

HERBS: we have specified when to use fresh or dried herbs. If substituting dried herbs for fresh, use dried (not ground) herbs in the proportions of 1:4 for fresh herbs, e.g., 1 teaspoon dried herbs instead of 4 teaspoons (1 tablespoon) chopped fresh herbs.

HOI SIN SAUCE: is a thick sweet Chinese barbecue sauce made from salted black beans, onion and garlic.

ITALIAN SAUSAGES: large fresh pork sausages, lightly salted.

JALAPENO PEPPERS: hot chillies, available in brine in bottles and cans.

JAM: a preserve of sugar and fruit.

JUNIPER BERRIES: aromatic flavour; an ingredient of gin.

KUMARA: orange sweet potato.

LAMB: any cuts of lamb suitable for stewing are also suitable for casseroles.

Chump chop: the chump is the cut from just above the hind legs to the mid-loin section; it can be used as a piece for roasting, or cut into chops.

Cutlet: small, tender rib chop.

Diced: cubed lean meat.

Leg: from the hindquarter.

Neck chop: we used "best" neck chops.

Rack: row of cutlets.

Rolled shoulder: boneless section of the forequarter, rolled and secured with string or netting.

Shank: forequarter leg.

LARD: fat obtained from melting down and clarifying pork fat; available packaged.

LEAVES: we used dried leaves. Fresh leaves are available but the flavour varies slightly.

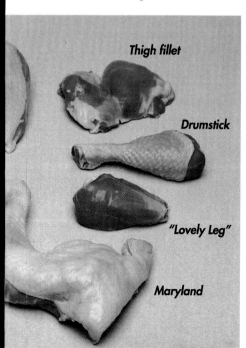

Thigh fillet

Drumstick

"Lovely Leg"

Maryland

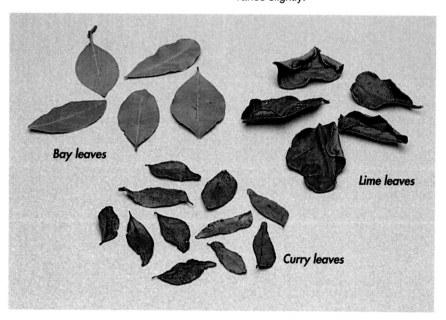

Bay leaves

Lime leaves

Curry leaves

LEMON GRASS: available fresh from Asian food stores.

MADEIRA: wine fortified with brandy.

MUSHROOMS:

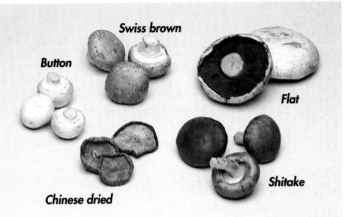

Button
Swiss brown
Flat
Shitake
Chinese dried

OIL:

Olive: a blend of refined and virgin olive oils, good for everyday cooking.

Peanut: made from ground peanuts, is the most commonly-used oil in Asian cooking; however, a lighter, salad type of oil can be used.

Sesame: an oil made from roasted, crushed white sesame seeds, used for flavouring.

Vegetable: we used a polyunsaturated vegetable oil.

ONION:

Red Spanish: large purplish-red onion.

Spring onions: vegetables with small white bulbs and long green leaves.

PANCETTA: cured pork belly; bacon can be substituted.

PEPPERONI: sausage made of minced pork and beef with added fat; flavoured with hot red pepper.

PEPPERS: capsicum or bell peppers.

PLUM SAUCE: a dipping sauce made of plums, sugar, chillies and spices.

POLENTA: usually made from ground corn (maize); similar to cornmeal but coarser and darker in colour. One can be substituted for the other but results will be slightly different.

PORK: any cuts of pork suitable for stewing are also suitable for casseroles.

Forequarter chops: from the shoulder area.

Neck: boneless cut.

PRAWNS: shrimp.

PROSCIUTTO: uncooked, unsmoked, cured ham; ready to eat when bought.

PRUNES: whole dried plums.

PUFF PASTRY, READY-ROLLED: frozen sheets of puff pastry available from supermarkets.

SAMBAL OELEK (also ulek or olek): a salty paste made from ground chillies.

SCALLOPS: we used the scallops with coral (roe) attached.

SEASONED PEPPER: a combination of black pepper, sugar and bell pepper.

SEMOLINA: a hard part of the wheat which is sifted out and used mainly for making pasta.

SESAME SEEDS: there are 2 types, black and white; we used the white variety in this book.

To toast: spread seeds evenly onto oven tray, toast in moderate oven for about 5 minutes or stir over heat in heavy-based pan until golden brown.

SHALLOTS:

Green: also known as scallions, spring onions and eschalots.

SNOW PEAS: also known as mange tout (eat all).

SPINACH, ENGLISH: a soft-leafed vegetable, more delicate in taste than silverbeet (Swiss chard); young silverbeet can be substituted for English spinach.

STAR ANISE: the dried star-shaped fruit of an evergreen tree. It is used sparingly in Chinese cooking and has an aniseed flavour.

SUGAR: we used coarse granulated table sugar, also known as crystal sugar, unless otherwise specified in our recipes.

Brown: a soft fine granulated sugar containing molasses which gives its characteristic colour.

Caster: also known as superfine; is fine granulated table sugar.

Palm: fine sugar from the coconut palm. It is sold in cakes, also known as gula jawa, gula melaka and jaggery. Palm sugar can be substituted with brown or black sugar.

TABASCO SAUCE: made with vinegar, hot red peppers and salt.

TAMARIND SAUCE: if unavailable, soak about 30g dried tamarind in a cup of hot water, stand 10 minutes, squeeze pulp as dry as possible and use the flavoured water.

TOMATO:

Paste: a concentrated tomato puree used in flavouring soups, stews, sauces and casseroles, etc.

Puree: canned pureed tomatoes (not tomato paste). Use fresh, peeled, pureed tomatoes as a substitute, if preferred.

Tomato Supreme: a canned product consisting of tomatoes, onions, celery, peppers, cheese and seasonings.

VEAL: the meat from a very young calf, which can be identified by its pale pink flesh.

Chop: from the rib and loin (back).

Cutlet: choice chop from the mid-loin (back) area.

Diced: cubed lean meat.

Forequarter: area containing neck, shoulder and ribs.

Loin chop: from the loin (back) area.

Nut: a lean cut of meat from the leg.

Osso bucco: this famous Italian dish uses the hind or forequarter shank or knuckle cut into medallions. When the knuckle is trimmed of meat at the thin end, this is known as a "Frenched" knuckle.

Shoulder: from the forequarter.

Steak: schnitzel.

VINEGAR: we used both white and brown malt vinegar.

Balsamic: originated in the province of Modena, Italy. Regional wine is specially processed then aged in antique wooden casks to give a pungent flavour.

Red wine: is based on red wine.

White: made from spirit of cane sugar.

ZUCCHINI: courgette.

MAKE YOUR OWN STOCK

If you prefer to make your own stock, these recipes can be made up to 4 days ahead and stored, covered, in the refrigerator. Be sure to remove any fat from the surface after the cooled stock has been refrigerated overnight. If the stock is to be kept longer, it is best to freeze it in smaller quantities. Stock is also available in cans or tetra packs. Be aware of their salt content. Stock cubes or powder can be used. As a guide, 1 teaspoon of stock powder or 1 small crumbled stock cube mixed with 1 cup (250ml) water will give a fairly strong stock. Be aware of the salt and fat content of stock cubes and powders.

BEEF STOCK
2kg meaty beef bones
2 medium (300g) onions
2 sticks celery, chopped
2 medium (250g) carrots, chopped
3 bay leaves
2 teaspoons black peppercorns
5 litres (20 cups) water
3 litres (12 cups) water, extra

Place bones and unpeeled chopped onions in baking dish. Bake in hot oven about 1 hour or until bones and onions are well browned. Transfer bones and onions to large pan, add celery, carrots, bay leaves, peppercorns and water, simmer, uncovered, 3 hours. Add extra water, simmer, uncovered, further 1 hour; strain.

FISH STOCK
1.5kg fish bones
3 litres (12 cups) water
1 medium (150g) onion, chopped
2 sticks celery, chopped
2 bay leaves
1 teaspoon black peppercorns

Combine all ingredients in large pan, simmer, uncovered, 20 minutes; strain.

CHICKEN STOCK
2kg chicken bones
2 medium (300g) onions, chopped
2 sticks celery, chopped
2 medium (250g) carrots, chopped
3 bay leaves
2 teaspoons black peppercorns
5 litres (20 cups) water

Combine all ingredients in large pan, simmer, uncovered, 2 hours; strain.

VEGETABLE STOCK
2 large (360g) carrots, chopped
2 large (360g) parsnips, chopped
4 medium (600g) onions, chopped
12 sticks celery, chopped
4 bay leaves
2 teaspoons black peppercorns
6 litres (24 cups) water

Combine all ingredients in large pan, simmer, uncovered, 1½ hours; strain.

All stock recipes make about 2.5 litres (10 cups).

Index

QUICK CONVERSION GUIDE

Wherever you live in the world you can use our recipes with the help of our easy-to-follow conversions for all your cooking needs. These conversions are approximate only. The difference between the exact and approximate conversions of liquid and dry measures amounts to only a teaspoon or two, and will not make any difference to your cooking results.

MEASURING EQUIPMENT

The difference between measuring cups internationally is minimal within 2 or 3 teaspoons' difference. (For the record, 1 Australian metric measuring cup will hold approximately 250ml.) The most accurate way of measuring dry ingredients is to weigh them. When measuring liquids use a clear glass or plastic jug with metric markings.

If you would like the measuring cups and spoons as used in our Test Kitchen, turn to page 128 for details and order coupon. In this book we use metric measuring cups and spoons approved by Standards Australia.

● a graduated set of four cups for measuring dry ingredients; the sizes are marked on the cups.
● a graduated set of four spoons for measuring dry and liquid ingredients; the amounts are marked on the spoons.
● 1 TEASPOON: 5ml.
● 1 TABLESPOON: 20ml.

NOTE: NZ, CANADA, USA AND UK ALL USE 15ml TABLESPOONS.
ALL CUP AND SPOON MEASUREMENTS ARE LEVEL.

DRY MEASURES

METRIC	IMPERIAL
15g	½oz
30g	1oz
60g	2oz
90g	3oz
125g	4oz (¼lb)
155g	5oz
185g	6oz
220g	7oz
250g	8oz (½lb)
280g	9oz
315g	10oz
345g	11oz
375g	12oz (¾lb)
410g	13oz
440g	14oz
470g	15oz
500g	16oz (1lb)
750g	24oz (1½lb)
1kg	32oz (2lb)

LIQUID MEASURES

METRIC	IMPERIAL
30ml	1 fluid oz
60ml	2 fluid oz
100ml	3 fluid oz
125ml	4 fluid oz
150ml	5 fluid oz (¼ pint/1 gill)
190ml	6 fluid oz
250ml	8 fluid oz
300ml	10 fluid oz (½ pint)
500ml	16 fluid oz
600ml	20 fluid oz (1 pint)
1000ml (1 litre)	1¾ pints

WE USE LARGE EGGS WITH AN AVERAGE WEIGHT OF 60g

HELPFUL MEASURES

METRIC	IMPERIAL
3mm	⅛in
6mm	¼in
1cm	½in
2cm	¾in
2.5cm	1in
5cm	2in
6cm	2½in
8cm	3in
10cm	4in
13cm	5in
15cm	6in
18cm	7in
20cm	8in
23cm	9in
25cm	10in
28cm	11in
30cm	12in (1ft)

HOW TO MEASURE

When using the graduated metric measuring cups, it is important to shake the dry ingredients loosely into the required cup. Do not tap the cup on the bench, or pack the ingredients into the cup unless otherwise directed. Level top of cup with knife. When using graduated metric measuring spoons, level top of spoon with knife. When measuring liquids in the jug, place jug on flat surface, check for accuracy at eye level.

OVEN TEMPERATURES

These oven temperatures are only a guide; we've given you the lower degree of heat. Always check the manufacturer's manual.

	C° (Celsius)	F° (Fahrenheit)	Gas Mark
Very slow	120	250	1
Slow	150	300	2
Moderately slow	160	325	3
Moderate	180 – 190	350 – 375	4
Moderately hot	200 – 210	400 – 425	5
Hot	220 – 230	450 – 475	6
Very hot	240 – 250	500 – 525	7

TWO GREAT OFFERS FROM THE AWW HOME LIBRARY

Here's the perfect way to keep your Home Library books in order, clean and within easy reach. More than a dozen books fit into this smart silver grey vinyl folder. PRICE: Australia $11.95; elsewhere $21.95; prices include postage and handling. To order your holder, see the details below.

All recipes in the AWW Home Library are created using Australia's unique system of metric cups and spoons. While it is relatively easy for overseas readers to make any minor conversions required, it is easier still to own this durable set of Australian cups and spoons (photographed). PRICE : Australia: $5.95; New Zealand: $A8.00; elsewhere: $A9.95; prices include postage & handling.
This offer is available in all countries.

TO ORDER YOUR METRIC MEASURING SET OR BOOK HOLDER:

PHONE: Have your credit card details ready. **Sydney:** (02) 260 0035; **elsewhere in Australia:** 008 252 515 (free call, Mon-Fri, 9am-5pm) or *FAX* your order to (02) 267 4363 or *MAIL* your order by photocopying or cutting out and completing the coupon below.

PAYMENT: **Australian residents:** We accept the credit cards listed, money orders and cheques. **Overseas residents:** We accept the credit cards listed, drafts in $A drawn on an Australian bank, also English, New Zealand and U.S. cheques in the currency of the country of issue.
Credit card charges are at the exchange rate current at the time of payment.

Please photocopy and complete coupon and fax or send to:
AWW Home Library Reader Offer, ACP Direct, PO Box 7036, Sydney 2001.

❏ Metric Measuring Set   ❏ Holder

Please indicate number(s) required.

Mr/Mrs/Ms _____

Address _____

_____

Postcode _____ Country _____

Ph: ( ) _____ Bus. Hour:_____

I enclose my cheque/money order for $ _____ payable to ACP Direct

OR: please charge my:

❏ Bankcard ❏ Visa ❏ MasterCard ❏ Diners Club ❏ Amex

☐☐☐☐☐☐☐☐☐☐☐☐☐☐☐☐ Exp. Date ___/__

Cardholder's signature_____

(Please allow up to 30 days for delivery within Australia. Allow up to 6 weeks for overseas deliveries.)
Both offers expire 30/12/95.   AWSF95